JOSIP LONČAR

THE MYSTERY OF
THE HOLY EUCHARIST

DEEPENING OUR UNDERSTANDING TOWARD
A MORE REVERENT PARTICIPATION AT MASS

Foreword by Cardinal Vinko Puljić

Original title: Sveta misa. Najsvetiji događaj na svijetu

Publisher: Figulus Media, Koprivnica,

www.figulus-media.com

Author: Josip Lončar

Theological Approval: Fr. Antonio-Mario Čirko, OCD, Ph.D

ISBN 979-885-1719-26-4

CIP designation is accessible in the computerised catalogue National and University library in Zagreb under the code number 0010395668.

Scripture quotations are taken from the New Revised Standard Version (NRSV) of The Holy Bible, unless otherwise stated.

CONTENTS

Fulfill, Lord, the promise of Your Son:

May the Holy Spirit lead us into the mystery of this sacrifice and open us to all truth.

(From the Offertory prayers on the Feast of Pentecost.)

FOREWORD...

THE EUCHARIST – THE LEGACY JESUS LEFT US

In July this year (2019), the book by Josip Lončar, *The Holy Mass: the Holiest Phenomenon in the World[1]*, was given to me to write a few words as a foreword on the occasion of its second edition. At the beginning of the book, the author thanks everyone who supported him in the preparation and publication of this book. When I read the encouragement of his Bishop for him to grow in love towards God, the Church, and mankind, I wanted to be part of that support as well.

It makes me happy that a layman is writing about the Eucharist with so much love that he wishes to inspire others to value and live from that "holiest reality on the face of the earth."

Jesus, before offering His sacrifice of blood on Calvary, provided the means for this same sacrifice to be repeated in a sacramental manner and left it to us with the words: "Do this in remembrance of me" (Lk. 22:19). In his meditations, the author draws from *the Sacred Scripture* and *the Catechism of the Catholic Church*, as well as other documents, to help others comprehend the holiness of that event. In order to be able to recognise, experience and live this holiest event on earth; we have to prepare for it. A well-prepared soul can experience the holiness of this act and obtain manifold fruits from it. On this earth, there is no holier event than the celebration of the Holy Eucharist, which both wells up and overflows powerful stimulation over both our personal life and our life in the community.

Even we, ordinary people, when we must depart from this world and leave our dear ones, we leave behind our words in a letter or we leave objects to remind them of us in the best way we know, in order *to continue to be present for them.* So did Jesus. He wanted to be and to remain in this act for all those for whom He suffered, died, and rose again. For that reason, He instituted this wonderful gift in which He perpetuates the very act of continual redemption and salvation. The author in this

---

1 This is the English translation of the title of the book as published in Croatia

work wants to help the reader to become conscious of that gift. First of all, to recognise this reality and then to practice and live this holiest of encounters between us mortal men and our immortal Redeemer.

I want to thank him for this effort and his words, with which he tried to help people perceive the Eucharist, to love it and to live this wonderful gift from Heaven to this world. May the Risen One who lives in the Eucharist give life to our faith for as long as we live, until we experience His promise that "one may eat of it and not die."

Sarajevo, on the Feast day of Bl. Miroslav Bulešič,

Cardinal Vinko Puljić,

Metropolitan Archbishop of Vrhbosna

INTRODUCTION

Lord, may this sacrifice bring continuous blessing. What the visible represents may be realised by the power of Your Spirit. Through Christ.

(Prayer over the gifts at Mass)

ALL CELEBRATIONS OF THE HOLY MASS are directed towards entering a communion: towards the partaking of the Sacrificial Lamb, towards a unity with Him within our own hearts, towards a unification of our prayers with Jesus, the Lamb, to the Father, towards a dwelling within Him (CCC 1382). The parts of the Mass are steps by which we climb upwards towards God and then we descend into our own hearts.

In every element of the Mass, we cooperate with the Holy Spirit and we are guided by Him.

The Mass leads us into the presence of the Trinity, it leads us into Jesus' redeeming sacrifice, in which we participate by offering up the Eucharistic sacrifice and receiving the Lamb. By this participation, Jesus enters into us in communion, so that we can enter in Him. The deeper we enter into Him, the closer we will feel His presence, and the greater our benefit and joy will be.

At the Holy Mass, we will receive as much grace as we have, with the help of His Spirit, opened to and disposed our hearts towards it (CCC 1128). The Church is quite right to warn us that "these dispositions are the precondition both for the reception of other graces conferred in the celebration itself and the fruits of new life which the celebration is intended to produce afterwards" (CCC 1098).

Closeness to God during the Holy Mass depends first and foremost on our desire, on the will of our spirit, and on our heart. The closer we come to Him, the more we will be blessed, fulfilled and satisfied.

God wanted the Church and He wanted the liturgy. He wanted us to live in a community of people and that we glorify Him together. He wanted us to depend on one another and He wanted us to love one another.

The Holy Mass offers every one of us the dignity to live as sons or daughters of God. The commemoration of Jesus' sacrifice for our needs makes us healthier in our souls and spirits and contributes to our wholeness as people. Offering the Holy Mass for the needs of others makes our life more worth living.

The first part of the book underlines, also with personal testimonies, the infinity of treasures found in the Holy Mass, and God's deep desire to make us actively partake of it and His longing desire to touch us through this sacrament.

The second part of the book is widely focused on prayers we can pray and meditate in order to prepare for the Eucharistic celebration; and there are different prayers to suit different intentions that we come with to the Holy Mass.

IS IT REALLY WORTHY GOING TO MASS?

I WROTE THIS BOOK PRIMARILY because I *love* to talk and write about the Mass, because I am deeply convinced that the Mass is the most important event in this world, but also because I believe that we do not speak enough about it, nor do we testify enough about its importance.

The book is aimed at anyone for whom, for whatever reason, the Mass has not become the deepest longing of the soul. If it has not become the true spiritual experience for you, the true fountain and centre of spirituality, then this book is definitely for you. In it, I have tried to present my own experience after years of searching, studying and meditating on the liturgy, as well as my own participation in the Mass over the years.

The title chosen for this book "The mystery of the Holy Eucharist - Deepening Our Understanding toward a more Reverent Participation at Mass" comes after I have noted that many people go to Mass and attend out of habit, often absent-minded and with an attitude of ticking the box of obligation.

Do we still believe that during Mass God is really present and works mysteriously, often in a silent way in our soul?

With a little effort, we can find many Church documents which offer us all the necessary information on participating fully and fruitfully, but those documents do not explain *how* to achieve this.

For example, such documents tell us that we *must* prepare if we want to participate *"fully and fruitfully"*, but do not tell us in what way. They tell us that *"our minds should be in harmony with our voices"* and we should *"cooperate with the fullness of grace"*, but in what way? Also, that *"how much we will receive depends very much on our disposition at the Holy Mass"* but we are not told whether this information is available somewhere nor how to attain that very disposition.

Therefore, it is difficult to find literature which gives a satisfactory answer to the question on *how* to work towards attaining these dispositions.

I am aware that the Holy Mass is an inexhaustible well for meditation and that there is so much more that I still have to discover and experience, but a part of what I have already discovered and experienced I wish to offer to you, my dear readers, for you to think about.

In this book, I concentrate on the redeeming sacrifice, in which we participate in the Mass, because I think this is an important theme which we do not talk enough about.

Jesus Christ participated completely in His sufferings: with His whole heart, His whole soul, His physical, mental and spiritual strength, and with all of His love. It was by His suffering, death and resurrection that He redeemed us because He loves us, He cares about us.

In the Holy Mass, we celebrate His redemption on our behalf: the mystery of His suffering, death, and resurrection. And the best way to celebrate this is to actively and effectively participate in this redemption. Our participation greatly depends on how well we know God, how much we love Him, and how much we care about our own salvation and the salvation of people close to us. If we really care and if we really want to draw on its temporal and spiritual fruits of redemption, then it will not be a problem to fulfill the requirements that the Church suggests. And we all find ourselves in various situations in life in which we really care and for which we are prepared to make particular sacrifices.

I am sad to admit that at certain times in my life there were Masses to which I just *went*. I never thought back then that I could use Jesus' sacrifice for myself or for anyone else; sincerely, with love and trust. And whenever I found myself in particular problems, I would put my trust in God, but only by means of some other devotions and prayers.

Since this book is aimed at ordinary people, I omitted long references to Old Testament sacrifices and in that way twenty or thirty pages were taken off this book. The Old Testament sacrifices are all fulfilled in Jesus' sacrifice and in every one of them we can find connections to the sacrifice of the Mass. I do not dwell too much on the Passover sacrifice because there is already a lot of literature available on the connections between it and the sacrifice of the Mass.

I am convinced that this book will be useful to those who find themselves in situations of need. We can put them all under the umbrella term of *situations where only God can help*. It will be very useful to those who are willing to stay close to those in need and be intercessors before God. But what would make me particularly happy is that some young man, having read it, should decide for the priesthood, and that some young woman would decide for the religious life.

However, in any case I would like for the reader to take from it whatever is useful for him or her or whatever applies to him or her.

(CCC 1098; CCC 1101; SC 11; CCC 133; CCC 1394; EE 11; CCC 1414; CCC 1246)

THREE KEY WORDS

A MARRIED COUPLE, WHO ARE dear friends of mine, were once invited as honoured guests to an opera performance unknown to them. Because of unavoidable obligations, they were delayed for a few minutes and so arrived not having had the time to read the libretto which would have acquainted them with the work and the events in it. To make things worse, as soon as the opera began, they realised to their unpleasant surprise that it was sung in a language unknown to them.

At its conclusion, which they anxiously awaited, they wanted to know how the others who were present had enjoyed the opera. They noticed different reactions from the public: it ranged from complete delight to withdrawal and declarations of boredom, and there were even some who had left before it ended.

While chatting about their experience, we somehow came to compare it with our participation in the Holy Mass. At Mass, we too can notice a range of reactions: from those who are bored, and to those who participate in it with undivided care and understanding at the level of their hearts. Of course, the importance of the Holy Mass is incomparably greater than that of the opera, but the comparison can bring us to specific conclusions. When people who enjoy opera, ballet, or some sport, work or hobby, and participate in an activity with interest, understanding, and undivided attention, there is always someone whose passion is contagious, who ignites the passion in the hearts of others, and who, in a positive sense, "contaminates" them. The same goes for the majority of those who participate in the Mass actively and fruitfully with understanding and undivided devotion.

Here, we have arrived at the first two key words: to *convey* and to *implant*.

All of us had various teachers, including religion teachers during our school years. In some subjects, we had to settle for teachers who were *only* giving us their knowledge of the subject. However there were others who gave us not only their knowledge, but also experience and love towards the subject they taught, and others who managed to ignite us with their passion about the subject. I can remember a priest who sparked our interest in the Holy Mass to the point that we all knew parts of the Mass by heart. "Celebrating the Mass" was the most favourite game for us!

This, coupled with the example of our parents and grandparents, consolidated in us a need for and a love for the Holy Mass. They communicated to us enough understanding about it as was suitable to our age and level of maturity.

As I explained in the example above, my friends were opera enthusiasts, but understood virtually nothing about this particular opera, although they know much about operas in general. If they had prepared, read the libretto, discussed it with others, acquainted themselves with all its important elements, they would have had a completely different experience.

Here, we come to the third key word: *preparation*. This term presupposes *studying the elements of the Mass* and preparing oneself individually *for every single Mass*. Our disposition towards participation depends completely on our *preparation* for the Mass.

IT IS IMPORTANT TO KNOW

GOD IS CONSTANTLY WITH US, from the moment when we became His thought, because of His love. However, just because God is always with us, it does not necessarily mean that *we* are with Him (CCC 30).

Even though we became His children through baptism and a temple of the Holy Spirit, we are with God only when we truly desire to be, when we really want to spend our time in His presence, when we want to meet Him in the temple, the temple of our own hearts.

God will not force us to come to Him. It is possible to be in the church, to be at Mass, it is also possible to spend a number of hours saying prayers, and at the same time not to be with Him or in Him.

We enter into God's presence only when, with undivided attention, we direct our thoughts, our words, our desires, our thanksgiving, our trust, our worries, our hopes, our consciousness: our hearts and minds to Him.

When we completely concentrate on the Lord, He can absorb our attention so that we are no longer limited by this world and we can actually enter into His presence. Many of the faithful have had this experience. It can happen during praise, during a reading of the Word of God, during Eucharistic adoration. Our Lord can draw us so strongly into His presence that we cease to be aware of the passing of time or the outward impulses of our body (heat or cold, pain, hunger, thirst, tiredness, sleepiness...). Instead, we become conscious of a deep inner peace, of God's goodness and gentleness. We become aware of the meaning of words which we listen to and which we pronounce.

Why is it that many of the church goers do not experience this at the Holy Mass? Maybe it is because no one has ever testified, or communicated, or shared their experience. Maybe it is because we never understood with our minds, nor recognised with our hearts that the time spent at the Holy Mass could be pleasant and fruitful. Maybe because we do not prepare for the Mass the way we could or we should?

We live our lives in the world and in God. Everyone decides for themselves how much time they want to spend with God. When we are with Him, His all-empowering grace is at our disposition. And just as the vine cannot bear fruit without those juices which are drawn from the roots, in the same way we cannot do anything without Jesus, without His grace – which is active only when we are *with Him and in Him*. Without Jesus, we cannot believe with our hearts, we cannot forgive from the heart (CCC 154). Without Him, we cannot resist (at least not completely) the drives of the flesh, the devil, and the world. Without Him, we cannot be freed or healed to our very hearts. Without Him, we cannot make progress in faith, hope, and love. Without Him, we cannot either accept or bring forth any of that (Jn. 15:1-5).

We, Christians, we can *live in God's presence and enjoy it* in a special way.

If we are born from above, of the Holy Spirit, then we are not enslaved by rituals. We are not bound by any particular fixed prayers, but rather by the need to always try to seek the right "therapy" – the right food for whatever is needed at a given time.

There are times when I read and meditate on *The Sacred Scripture*, times when I pray and meditate on the rosary, times when I read a good spiritual book, times when the Psalms delight me, times when I meditate on the Passion of Jesus, and times in which I praise, bless, and thank Him. Each of these times can last from a couple of hours to a couple of months. I always try and seek out whatever formula allows me to *enjoy the presence of God.* When I say "enjoy", I mean that I always feel good, accepted and loved when I am with God. This, of course, does not mean I will always feel joy. When I meditate on the Passion, I do not feel joy, but I can freely say that I enjoy it, because I know that I am returning love for Love.

I sometimes have days when prayer does not attract me in any way. On those days, I can always concentrate on doing someone some good with great care. When doing acts of mercy, I also enjoy God's presence. I feel that, in some way, I am giving back to Jesus something that He gave me.

These things which I mentioned happen at every Holy Mass. Every Holy Mass contains those forms of devotion and that's why the Mass is the most superb food and the most excellent therapy for our souls.

This is why I would not miss the Mass. I do not even want to miss the daily Mass – except in exceptional situations.

The Holy Mass is an encounter with God and a dwelling in Him in the fullest sense of the word. During Mass, we thank Him, we bless Him, we glorify Him, we adore Him, we confess our faith, we partake of His Body and Blood. We unite ourselves with Him. We present our needs to Him, and the needs of others, we listen to His Word, we learn from Him. At the time of the Mass, we participate in His sacrifice which redeems us from sins, weaknesses, sickness, pain...all that actually happens if and when we are in Him!

When our consciousness is focused on Him, and on the words that we are pronouncing and listening to, then we are in God. After this, when we return our thoughts to this world, to our daily obligations and concerns, grace is still with us and in us. Our inner self is conscious of God being with us and we remain in Him capable of living a supernatural divine life. When we notice that we do not have enough strength to forgive, to tolerate, to give, when our inner peace is gone, when we have lost our joy, we reenter God and spend some more quality time in Him, and refill ourselves with His very necessary grace for living.

To some of us, Sunday Mass is not enough, solely because we have tasted just how different our day is when we start with the Holy Mass, and what it is like when we do not.

(Ps. 139:1-18; CCC 1265; Rom. 8:5-12; CCC 368; CCC 94; CCC 157; CCC 1743)

THE HOLY MASS IS
THE SACRAMENT OF REDEMPTION[2]

Whenever we celebrate the memory of this sacrifice, part of our redemption is completed; and so let us worthily celebrate this mystery. Through Christ.

(Offertory prayer)

---

2 I have chosen to use the term Redemption, rather than Salvation, to emphasise some aspects. While persons need to respond to God's grace and accept Jesus Christ as Saviour and Lord to be saved, let us remember that it was God's initiative to provide the full redemption through the incarnation, life, death, resurrection and ascension of His Son, Jesus Christ. Salvation comes from salvus, which means to be healthy, to be well, to be fulfilled whereas Redemption comes from to redeem, to free from slavery (as in the old times when slaves obtained their freedom when someone paid a ransom for their release). This is what Jesus did by offering himself as a victim in our place and to make men and women free from sin. and from the seductions of evil, in order to be able to respond actively to the grace of salvation. Redemption has therefore a broader concept than that of salvation. We are saved when we accept redemption. (see International Theological Commission, Some questions on the theology of God the Redeemer issued by the Vatican, October 1995)

On Holy Thursday, Jesus gave us the sacrament of the Eucharist as a means by which we can actively and fruitfully participate in His redemption and receive spiritual and temporal benefits from it; which we are entitled to for our redemption.

Through the sacrament of baptism, we are redeemed of original sin and of all sins which we have committed since then. Our sins are forgiven and we continue to receive forgiveness through the sacrament of Confession. However, we still have problems in some areas because of our tendency to sin which we cannot overcome. In the same way, sometimes we are overcome with addictions, severe or incurable ills, fears, depression...

The prophet Isaiah, who lived seven centuries before Jesus' earthly life, saw Jesus dying on the cross in a vision. He was able to see what Christ won for us; humanity. Isaiah quite rightly asked how many from his own times, and how many people from the future, would be able to believe and trust in the spiritual and temporal merits which belong to us as a result of Jesus' redeeming sacrifice on the cross and also through the offering of the Holy Mass (Is. 53:1,4-6).

And sadly the answer is: too few. Many "cultural" Catholics do not understand how to actively participate in the celebration of His passion, death and resurrection because they treat the Mass as a ritual and often do not enter into the mystery of the Mass. And often this is not their fault. However why do we not believe that if 2000 years ago "the people all tried to touch him, because power was coming from him and healing them all" (Lk. 6:19) why should not this happen more frequently also today when Jesus is *the same yesterday, today and forever*? We should go to Mass with expectant faith!

(LG 3; EE 11; EE 12; CCC 1382; Is. 53:1,4-6)

GOD'S PLAN FOR MANKIND

It is hard to understand the sacrifice of the Mass in which we participate without understanding the plan of God for man (CCC 280).

God created man in his own image and likeness. He crowned him with glory and grace, He gave him authority over the land (Gen. 1:26; Ps. 8:6-9), and gave him life in abundance. He created man in order to share love and respect with him, in order for him to participate in His creation, in His managing and dominating the world, so that he can share in the joy of living.

In his earthly Heaven, Adam enjoyed God's presence and was happy in the mission that God entrusted to him. He gave him authority, power, knowledge, and wisdom. He lived life to the fullest. In Heaven, in eternity, we will enjoy God's presence even more, and I am convinced that we will enjoy the mission that we will have in His kingdom – we will enjoy the abundance of life.

Every human being is conceived and created as an eternal creature and no human being will cease to exist. God, even before our birth, gave us incredible possibilities which are beyond our recognition. He gave them to us not only for this life, but for the whole of eternity (CCC 1029). In the depths of our souls, He put the same gifts He gave to Adam. The Scriptures tell us that we are a miracle – made in the image and likeness of God.

The peak of our "miraculousness" is love. It is most clearly seen in the readiness to give up our lives for one another, when we consciously decide to suffer and even to die in order to save the lives of others (Jn. 15:13). Some discover this readiness within themselves only when they are in some specific life situations. For example, a mother in late pregnancy who, because of an incurable disease, has to decide who will live, she or her child. Or a man who is ready to risk his own life in order to save another who is in great danger. Or even a daughter-in-law who has to care for a mother-in-law with whom she has never been on good terms with, or a mother-in-law who, due to her illness, suddenly becomes disabled and bedridden for a long period of time.

Those people do not even consider if they are going to get something in return for this sacrifice! What then should we think about missionaries, people who go around doing good, about evangelists, priests, nuns, parents with very sick children or many others who have heard God's call, renounced themselves in order to live and die for others? Their joy is precisely in doing good regardless of what it costs them. Are they not miracles?

God gave us His Spirit so that we could discover with His help what has been implanted in us since the time of creation (1 Cor. 2:12) One good example of this is Mother Teresa of Calcutta. Before she dedicated herself to the dying on the streets of Calcutta, she was a respected nun and a highly educated teacher. Some of her students cared for the poor on the streets and spoke to sister Teresa about it, but the thought that she could do something about it was strange to her. She neither felt called nor capable of something like that. She didn't know back then in her heart that every man (including herself) is created with a miraculous capacity to make the greatest sacrifices in love for their fellow men. In a moment of grace, she recognised that truth and from then on, her life took on a completely different meaning and call.

One of the most important reasons why we have received the Holy Spirit is for Him to reveal to us the dignity of every man created in the image of God.

In the Garden of Eden (earthly Heaven), there were many trees, but in the centre there were two special ones: the tree of life and the tree of knowledge of good and evil. Man was allowed to eat from all of the trees except from the tree of the knowledge of good and evil. God had forbidden this, warning Adam that on that day, when he breaks that commandment, he will die (Gen. 2:15-17).

We, people, born of Adam and Eve, have to suppose that God explained to Adam what it means to die. If this were not true, His punishment would not have been just. Adam had no experience of death and that's why he *had to **trust** His Word* that death was exactly as God had described. Adam had no experience of God's judgements, which is why he *had to believe* that God in His justice and unbiasedness would have to stand by this terrifying threat, even though he knew Him as an infinitely good Father. Adam should have had a fear of God, he should have known that God would stand by His words. For as long as Adam believed God, he was saved: *he lived outside of sin* and he had eternal life.

We, people, born of Adam and Eve, do not have the experience of eternal life and that is why we **have to believe** the very God's word which tells us that we will live in eternity either in Heaven or in Hell. In the same way, **we must believe** when He tells us that He will be a just and unbiased judge and that, because of His justice and unbiasedness, many will have to be judged to Hell where, instead of eternal life, they will have eternal suffering.

God was able to see Adam's heart every time when Adam, with his free will, resisted the forbidden fruit, because it attracted him having been beautiful to the eye and desirable for his wisdom. He respected this resistance. Every day, Adam was exposed to temptation, because the tree was at the centre of the garden, at the centre of his attention, just like the tree of life from which he ate life. Our conscience functions in the same way: we are constantly in situations where we can choose good and avoid evil (CCC 1776-1802). We are often faced with an attractive tree, whose fruit can kill our faith and our desire for eternal life in Heaven.

What God wants for Adam and Eve is what He wants for everyone: He wants us to take His words very seriously. He wants them to be important and holy for us, and to believe them infinitely. God wants His word written in our hearts, because that is the only way to live in love, peace, and justice. Only in that way can we have the dignity of the children of God (CCC 1780-1782). Often, that is not easy, and precisely because it's not easy, we earn His respect (Jn. 12:26).

WHY DID GOD ALLOW ADAM TO SIN

WHY DID GOD ALLOW US to sin? Without free will, without the possibility to sin, without the possibility for us to choose between good and evil, we would be like robots. We would not be able to express our reverence for God or for anyone else for that matter. We would have no dignity, standing, or merit. In Heaven, in God's eternal kingdom, all those saved will be holy, but not everyone will be rewarded equally and in the same measure. The level of glory will not be the same but all will be filled with joy and without lacking anything. St Teresa of Avila gives the example of glasses: there are different sizes of glasses but each one may be fully filled to the brim and they will lack nothing.

We ourselves could not have decided how, when or where we would have been born into this earthly life, but with our life choices, with our free will, we can choose our position in eternity. We ourselves can continuously opt for love, respect, forgiveness, and doing good. Alone we can decide how much we want to sacrifice. Alone we decide if we want to progress in goodness, if we want to change, if we want to grow in grace and wisdom. That free decision (free will) is given to us, so that all of us could obtain our eternal position in a perfectly just and unbiased way, so that each one of us could gain our eternal standing. Every good thing that we do, even giving a glass of water to one of Christ's thirsty disciples, has a huge influence on our eternal destiny. (Mt. 10:42; Mk. 9:41). That is why, in this short life, we should try to increase our heavenly treasures (Lk. 6:23; Lk. 6:35).

Adam and Eve loved God, but they loved themselves more, and therefore they did not honour Him to the fullest, which is why they did not fully believe Him. They did not possess that fear of God which was required (Mt. 16:24; Mk. 8:34: Lk. 9:23; Jn. 12:25). Then, one day, Satan interfered. Adam and Eve directed *too much attention to him and to the forbidden fruit* and he used that opportunity. He seduced them to desire what did not belong to them and led them to sin. They trusted and believed the serpent whom God has called a liar and deceiver. They decided to revolt and become equal to God. They wished to break free and no longer depend on God, having to live by His rules. *They wished to enjoy life even more.* Does this sound familiar? They sinned and altered their standing before God, they renounced their dignity. They lost access to the tree of life and were driven out of the heavenly garden. The loss of grace made them tend towards sin, toward fear, pain and sickness, physical death, and afterwards, what is much worse – eternity in Hell awaited them. This would not have happened had they loved God more than themselves, if they had been grateful, and had they respected Him and feared Him.

Satan, the true lord of all those who belong to the world and not to God, still applies the same tactics and in them we have a perpetuation of the original battle (1 Jn. 5:19; Eph. 6:10-20).

Expelled Adam did not long for health, or for wealth, nor for anything that we might consider commodities in this life, because nothing here could compare with what he had experienced in paradise. He was grateful for what he had, but above all he longed for God, for friendship with Him, for everything that he used to do in paradise. He longed for his incredibly high dignity which he had lost.

Many generations have passed by since Adam and Eve, but man is still driven by the feeling of having been rejected from paradise, rejected by God. We are born, we live and die in a highly unjust world. In the depths of our souls, we crave for the peace and dignity that Adam enjoyed in paradise, a foretaste of which many of us experience in the presence of God, when we dwell in Him. The deeper we enter God, the more conscious we become of those yearnings. The devil, the flesh, and the world, all have their own version of happiness, peace, and dignity. They offer us abundance of life if we just turn our back on God. God, on the other hand, offers us His own version of the fullness of life exemplified in the earthly life of His Son, but also in the lives of many saints. One of the convicts crucified with Jesus looked at the dying Jesus and His Mother beneath the cross, while the other convict looked at the crowd who were insulting him. One had trust in Jesus and the other trusted in this world (Lk. 23:39-43). *It depends on us who we are going to look up to, because whomever we look up to, most often, that is whom we believe.*

And that is how it will be until Jesus comes again.

THE GOOD NEWS

ADAM AND EVE WERE SURE that they had lost Heaven irrevocably. And they knew very well what they had lost. God knew that man would sin and die, but He allowed it because He knew that from his fall he could actually gain an even greater blessing than which he had before the fall (CCC 280, 302, 412).

God, first of all, announces the Gospel to Adam. He announces the possibility of salvation, the possibility of, through faith in the redemptive sacrifice of His only begotten Son Jesus Christ, he could be born again into the life that he had lost (CCC 55 and 410). After Adam, God unceasingly announces the same Good News to Abraham, Moses, Isaiah, and other prophets (1 Pt. 1:10-12; Is. 53:1-2; Lk. 2:25-38; Jn. 8:56; CCC 522).

God did not completely abandon Adam. Even though Adam and Eve had been cast out of paradise, they still lived before the face of God (in His presence) and they communicated with Him (Gen. 4:16). Can we even imagine Adam at the moment when God told him that there was a way in which his offence could be forgiven, and that he could be saved, and that he could be reborn for Heaven (Jn. 3:3)? For Adam, the Gospel was certainly good and joyful news. It was the best possible news he could hear.

God reported to Adam that his sin could be forgiven and that he could once again be born for Heaven, but that the guilt for his wrongs would have to be put on the back of someone else. Someone else would have to die innocent so that Adam could be forgiven and so he could be born once again (Is. 53:12).

That someone else is Jesus, God's own Son. That punishment He took freely upon Himself (Is. 53:1-12).

Was Adam able to accept this? He could have been because he knew that Jesus would do this freely, out of deep love for mankind (Jn. 3:16). Adam could accept that Jesus would die in his place, because God had told him that His Son would not stay in the tomb, but would rise from the dead on the third day. How many people are there today that cannot accept the reality that they will be saved if they just accept that truth?!

Adam sinned and all those who are born of him suffer the consequences of his sin. Since we are not responsible for that original sin of Adam, God didn't intend that we ourselves pay the indemnity. He offered to pay it for all of us, all by Himself.

At the moment when Adam understood God's offer of salvation, he must have wept with his face in the ground in deep remorse, gratitude and respect.

WHAT HAS ADAM, OUR FIRST PARENT, TO DO WITH THE MASS?

ADAM'S SACRIFICE IS NOT NOTED anywhere in the Scriptures. What we do know for sure is that Adam continued to communicate with God after he was cast out of the garden of Eden and that God taught him to offer sacrifices. It is logical to suppose that God taught him the significance of those sacrifices. However, God offered to do His part, while Adam, asking forgiveness and reconciliation with Him, had to do his own. He had to offer up sacrifices of atonement for his sin – he had to offer up unblemished animals. He had to acknowledge his sin, seek forgiveness, put his hand on the head of the animal and so symbolically part with his guilt, slaughter the animal, and spill its blood. But that was not enough. Adam **had to believe** that this sacrifice, this ritual was only a sign, a spiritual link with the sacrifice in which Christ, the Lamb of God without blemish, would be killed. I am deeply convinced that Adam **had to believe** that by the ritual of sacrificing animals, he was, in some spiritual way, participating in the sacrifice of the Son of God which would happen when the time was ripe. *He had to believe* that laying his hands on that animal, in a spiritual reality, he was laying hands on the crucified Christ and was passing his sins onto Him so that He would pay the price in his stead (Is. 53:4-5).

If Adam did not believe in Jesus' sacrifice, then the sacrifice of animals would not have been effective, nor would any other ritual. Adam was saved because he believed that by sacrificing animals he was participating in Jesus' sacrifice, before it actually happened. If Jesus had given up on His sacrifice in the garden of Gethsemane, Adam's sin would not have been forgiven, because the blood of an animal cannot atone for sin. Jesus did not give up on His sacrifice and Adam was saved (Sir. 49:16).

It is important to notice the connection between the Old Testament and Jesus' sacrifice. That connection is *faith*. Those who offered atonement for sin had to believe that, by offering an animal sacrifice, they were participating in the Messianic (Christ's, the anointed one) sacrifice. The sacrifice they offered, no matter how much it meant to them in any way, could not atone for sin in itself. That sacrifice was always only a ritual, which, by faith, would connect them with the sacrifice of Jesus Christ. It was a means by which they could participate many times in advance, in Jesus' sacrifice which took place only once in history.

This mystery was hidden from the majority of Old Testament characters because they were not able to or they did not want to believe in that which God wanted to reveal to them through the prophets. But God did not condemn those who brought sacrifices of atonement before Him with a sincere heart, nor those who, because they were unaware, could not believe in Jesus' redemption. Moreover, He sent his Son after His death into the bowels of the earth and to those who were waiting in Sheol for redemption. He announced His sacrifice so that they could trust Him and be saved by faith (*Apostles' Creed*: "...he descended into Hell and on the third day rose again").

THE HOLY MASS AND I?

WE TOO HAVE TO OFFER up Jesus' sacrifice for redemption and salvation to the Father. The Eucharist is the means which Jesus instituted, so that we would be able to really participate multiple times in a spiritual, sacramental way – in His sacrifice which took place only once. So, just as Adam and the Old Testament people through the manifold sacrifices of animals participated in Jesus' sacrifice *ahead of its actual happening in time*, so too, can we, also participate in the same sacrifice multiple times celebrating the Eucharist *after its actual happening in time.*

How can we envisage this? When Jesus died on the cross, the Father saw the whole history of man before His eyes. He saw you and me and saw every single offering of Jesus' passion. Even though we will offer the sacrifice of the Mass many times during our life for different intentions, He already saw all of our offerings back then – at the actual moment of Jesus' passion and death. Which is why, all the things we handed over to Jesus and which we will hand over to Him in the future *to take upon Himself,* Jesus had already *taken it and carried it all* (Is. 53:4-5). When at Holy Mass we offer up His sacrifice to the Father, we have to be aware that this event takes place out of time.

The heavenly Father expects of us that we offer Jesus' sacrifice and, by doing so, receive His redemption, but also to intercede for others. Jesus wishes for us to receive His love through the offering of His sacrifice so that we receive as much spiritual and temporal goods as possible, both for ourselves and for others. Also, He wishes us to love Him back in the Eucharist. He wishes us to unite our sufferings with His own and, in that way, make up for what is missing in His sacrifice – and the only thing that is missing in His perfect offering is that we participate in it actively and fruitfully and that we intercede for others (Col. 1:24).

AND IF I DON'T HAVE FAITH?
THERE IS A SOLUTION!

WHY IS IT THAT TODAY we see so little concrete fruits of the Mass, i.e. temporal and spiritual benefits? There are a few reasons for this, but the main reason is inadequate preparation for the celebration of the Mass.

One of the most common reasons why we do not want to spend time or effort in the preparation for the Mass is that we do not understand the process of the growth of faith in our heart. Many lay people, and priests as well, sincerely recognise that they neither believe nor hope that they will be really listened to if they offer Jesus' sacrifice for some temporal and/or spiritual benefit. Probably no one ever testified to them nor did anyone "infect them" (in the positive sense) with faith.

I think that we can see the difference between faith based on understanding (intellectual faith) and faith from the heart. I mean, very few of us, with our own will, reject the biblical truth that God is our Father who created us out of love and who wants to look after us in everything. However, few people fully believe in that truth in their hearts. Or to put it differently, very few of us have had a real experience of the Father's love. Very few of us believers come before God as our beloved Father with our needs. We do not have the true full trust and faith that our prayer will be answered. Those who really dwell in the Father's presence are few.

While preparing to write this book, I read quite a lot of literature about the sacrifice of Mass. While doing so, I noticed that nearly all authors refer to the fifty-third chapter of the book of Isaiah, which speaks about Jesus' redemptive sacrifice, about Isaiah's suffering servant. But although Isaiah, while listing all that Jesus did for us (verses 4-5), mentions infirmities, diseases, transgressions, iniquities, including healing by His bruises, the authors almost dwell on sins. In the same way, they mention the Passover sacrifice, but they do not say that the fruit of the Passover sacrifice was the healing of all sick Jews. On that night, according to biblical reports, the highest number of healings ever, took place in the history of mankind (Ps. 105:37). They mention what they believe.

Many priests never even try to offer the sacrifice of the Mass for someone terminally ill (according to the rite of the Mass for the Sick), or to celebrate the Mass for the dying (according to the rite of the Mass for the Dying), precisely because they do not expect that God will really do something concrete. If they have expectant faith, then they would certainly do it. They will just excuse themselves saying: *Well, every Mass is for redemption.* If we really believe, then God can do whatever He wants, even when Masses are not offered according to the rites. Those particular rites are given to us precisely so that we can open ourselves up a little bit more, so that we can dispose our hearts a little more to receive, so that we can more readily accept redemption. It is for that reason, that these special rites were thought up.

If at least in our minds we accept that celebrating the sacrifice of the Mass is really participating in the act of redemption, we then have enough reason to express intentions with an expectation of them being heard. Holy words, acts, signs and symbols during the liturgical rite, lead us into various personal and community connections with God. And faith in the heart comes as a gift from God, out of a relationship with Him, as a response to our expectations. We may not receive that *faith of the heart* at the first experience of Mass, but rather as a result of continuous surrender to God over many Masses. This process of opening ourselves up to God's intervention in surrendering ourselves to His will can be called *expectation* because it is slightly different from just waiting. *Expectation* is the active participation in which, in the peace of our hearts, we are directed towards the Redeemer leaving it to Him to choose when redemption should take place and in what way. Expectation presupposes an absolute belief that God will act and that we are participating and will participate in that action.

Let us remember the example of the Old Testament prophets who were known to offer sacrifices continually in the expectation that God would speak to them (Num. 23:1-14). Let us remember Elijah when he prayed for rain. He expected rain even though there were no traces of clouds in the sky. He knew that the clouds would come as a result of his prayer, even though he did not know how long he would have to stay in praying to God. But that was not of prime importance because Elijah knew that for the duration of the prayer he would stand before God's face anyway. He knew that he would bask in His blessings, not only in the instant the prayer would be answered, but while he prayed to Him as well. We, like Elijah, should pray for our needs, regardless of the fact that many times afterwards, just like Elijah, we will look on cloudless skies. It is enough that we are obedient to God's commands like Elijah. It is enough that we participate in the Holy

Mass in expectation, enjoying His presence, and accepting all the graces that He gives us in our inner selves while we await an answer to our prayers. We must accept that sometimes redemption cannot come until we are freed and healed from the root cause of our problems and until we receive the necessary disposition to maintain and hold onto the answer to our prayers. Let us not be in a hurry, let us not be anxious about not receiving it immediately, but let us rather allow grace to prepare us so that we can value and preserve the grace when we receive it.

By doing so, faith of the heart will happen in an encounter with God. We do not necessarily have to have it before the start of the Mass.

GOD'S PLAN FOR THE LITURGY

GOD WANTED EVERY SACRIFICE TO be composed of certain acts, words, signs, and symbols. He sought liturgy in the first of Adam's sacrifices. He could have told Adam that it was enough to believe in Jesus' sacrifice which would take place in the future, to repent, and, in that way, receive salvation. But God did not want Adam to simply trust Him. He somehow wanted him to actively participate in the sacrifice. He wanted that the whole process, the whole rite – the choosing of the animal, the preparation of the animal, and everything else that was necessary for the offering – that it would serve for repenting and confessing of guilt. God wanted that the taking of the life of an innocent animal and the spilling of its blood would in an intimate way connect Him with the sacrifice of His son Jesus. Liturgy enables us in the most intimate way possible to connect with the crucified Christ, so that we participate actively, fully, and fruitfully.

We are born in original sin and fallen nature. At the moment of baptism (which God also sought as a liturgical act, a liturgical rite) and acceptance of faith, God forgives sins, breathes His Spirit into us and welcomes us back into His family as His children. At that moment, we are saved, but we still continue living in a body which displays a tendency towards sinfulness and in a world that the devil has power over. In every possible way, the enemy is trying to keep us away from God, to put us back under his authority and to tempt us away from the road of salvation.

At the moment of baptism, our fallen nature is not completely transformed into a new resurrected nature. We are still to a certain extent selfish and egocentric, and we feel rejected by God. We do not know Him well enough and we do not have a child-like trust in Him. We are not used to dwelling in His presence. Since our fallen nature still has a tendency towards sin and towards all the things the world is offering us, throughout our whole life we have to push ourselves towards our own conversion, against constant imbalances in our nature, and towards our growth in sanctity. This continued fertile conversion comes about through our dwelling within God, especially by redemption through the Eucharistic sacrifice.

We can only have peace, joy and freedom in those areas of our lives which are redeemed. This is why we will notice that with certain sins we don't have a problem, and that we even happily agree with God's commandments, while other sins we just can't seem to liberate ourselves from (Rom. 7:14-25). In the same way, we will notice that there are some of Jesus' words that we believe with our whole hearts, in others only with our understanding, while there are still other parts that we simply do not believe. There where we are not redeemed, we cannot have God's type of life. In that part of our nature, Jesus is not the Lord.

God wanted the Church, He wanted liturgy, He wanted sacraments, He wanted the Mass the way it is. He wanted us to eat His flesh and drink His blood. He wanted us to participate in His offering actively and fruitfully (Jn. 6: 50-59).

In the Passover sacrifice, the blood of the lamb was poured on the doorposts of the believing Jews, and the angel of death could not enter there to take the life of the firstborn children, nor the first born of their animals (Ex. 12:29). After eating on the sacrificed lamb, the Jews went from being slaves to being rich people (Ex. 12:35-36). All the sick, who ate the sacrificed lamb were healed (Ps. 105:37). They were healed so that they could walk towards the promised land.

While partaking of the flesh of the Lamb, with faith in our hearts, we too are healed in our spirits, our souls and bodies, so that we can successfully walk towards the promised lands, that is, towards God. By drinking His blood, over and over again, we renew the baptismal covenant in which God made us into His sons and daughters, in which we belong to Him and He looks after us.

Whoever eats Jesus' flesh and drinks His blood with faith in their hearts has life within them. What kind of life is Jesus talking about? That is a life in which we enjoy an intimate relationship with God. In God there is the fountain from which we drink and that is why Jesus gave His invitation that whoever is thirsty can come to the water, to come to Him, and to drink; whoever believes in Him, because in His blood is life, because in His blood is grace, because in His blood the Holy Spirit is powerfully present (Ps. 36:9; Jn. 7:37-39).

Jesus wishes that the sacrament of the Eucharist carries within itself a visible sign of drinking His consecrated blood, so that that sign in our hearts and heads calls to mind the source, the fountain of eternal life. In that way, He wished to dispose our hearts (our personal temple of the Holy Spirit) to fill us with the Spirit (Eph. 5:19). Jesus wanted us to drink His blood because He knew that His love can quench the thirst of our souls (CCC 1390).

We, Christians, the new people of God, do not offer animals, but rather participate in Jesus' sacrifice over and over again through the miracle of the Eucharist. When we celebrate the Eucharist, the memory of the death and resurrection of our Lord, that central event of salvation, becomes present in a real way and "completes the act of our redemption" (EE 11; LG 3; CCC 611).

Jesus Christ, while present in the Holy Mass, is the sacrifice, priest and altar : He sacrifices Himself, He presents our intentions to the Father with us, and He is the altar because we find ourselves in Him when we offer this sacrifice, or when at the Eucharist we become one with Him (CCC 1391). This is why eating on the Flesh of the Lamb and drinking His Blood is the peak of the Mass (CCC 1340 and 1128).

With baptism, we become priests, prophets and kings so that we can offer our intentions in the Mass in the form of Jesus' sacrifice, so that we can offer our own voluntary sacrifices built into that of Christ, offering them up for the redemption and salvation of sinners (Col. 1:24; CCC 783-784, 871, 1141, 1268, 1273, 1322).

At every Mass, we can offer up more intentions, together with the main Mass sacrifice of the community of the faithful, with the priest at its head. The number of intentions that we can offer will depend on how much faith we have in the Eucharist, and how much love we have towards those who need the graces from the cross.

I would go as far as to say that the liturgy of the Mass is conceived so that, through the Eucharist, we participate in Jesus' redeeming sacrifice in the most real and fruitful way. This is why I think that those who are responsible for the preparation of the Mass should dedicate the greatest possible attention to ensure that participation is as active and as fertile as possible.

For a more thorough understanding, I would at least, suggest reading and examining the section of the Catechism of the Catholic Church which speaks of the sacrament of the Eucharist (Second section, Chapter 3) and, of course, Ecclesia de Eucharistia (EE) of Saint Pope John Paul II.

THE GOODS WE CAN RECEIVE BY PARTICIPATING IN THE HOLY MASS

What are the benefits that we can receive? One of the biggest benefits of being and praying at Mass is of course the fact that both personally, and also as a community (parish), we can spend intense quality time with God and in God. We can thank Him for the good He gives us, we can praise and worship Him, we can intercede for others and for our own needs, we can listen to His Word, to His teaching, encouragement, direction, comfort and warnings... And, above all, we can participate actively, and fruitfully present to the Father the personal redemption or the redemption of others.

In the following section, I will list some of the goods that I personally most often encounter when offering the Mass for myself or for others.

(LG 3; EE 11; EE11; CCC 1382; Is. 53:1,4-5)

LIBERATION FROM PURGATORY

Almost every Mass which is not celebrated according to a special rite (Votive Masses) is offered for someone's liberation from purgatory. Souls who are destined for Heaven often go to purgatory because first they must atone for their unredeemed sins. In other words, sins which they were not sorry enough for, now need full purification in purgatory.

Through their suffering they perfect their love for God. Whoever has not reached perfection in love cannot enter Heaven.

Every one of us sins throughout our lives : in our thoughts, in our words, in the deeds we have done or in our omission to do good deeds. For some of those sins we have already atoned and so there is no need to worry about them at judgement. There are other sins we might have committed, admitted, and confessed, but in our hearts we did not have the proper degree of regret or sorrow. Some of the sins we even tried to justify. With some of our sins we deeply hurt others, but we did not have enough willpower or faith to atone for those sins. We sin very much, sometimes out of ignorance, because we simply do not dedicate enough time in order to get to know God and His holy Word. This is because we do not try to learn His commandments in their essence, which suppose love towards God, ourselves and our neighbour, and even towards our enemies. Only when we come to know the gravity of our sins can we truly repent. At the same time, God can only forgive us to the extent that we forgive those who have offended us (Mt. 18:23-35). Many souls go to purgatory simply because they did not forgive enough, even though they themselves wanted forgiveness.

The root of all sin is precisely in that we do not have enough will, or we do not show enough will to set up a lifelong intimate relationship with God. Because only with such a relationship can we really know Him in our hearts and love Him completely. Only with this love can we fruitfully love ourselves and others.

God with His love towards us is so merciful that He promised that even if we call on to Him at the moment of death, we will not be condemned to Hell (Rom. 10:13; Acts 2:21). However, many will have to spend a lot of time struggling and suffering in purgatory. The souls in purgatory cannot pray for themselves, but God is so merciful that He gave us the possibility to pray for them, and the most effective way to do that is by having Masses offered for them (CCC 1030-1032; CCC 1472).

SALVATION OF THE DYING

I BELIEVE THAT THE DYING are in great need of God's mercy, especially those who, for whatever reason, will die before old age. Fear of death, pain and disappointment provoked by the knowledge that their departure is too soon, fear for the family, feelings of rejection and helplessness, as well as the pain and discomfort of illness, are just some of the challenges which the dying person must face. Many of them are not in a state of grace, they do not live an intimate life with our Lord. God's word tells us that whoever calls out to the Lord will be saved : they will not end up in hell (Rom. 10:13). Many of the dying, especially those who experienced graces in their youth – for example, the experience of their first Holy Communion, or the experience of going to Mass with their parents when they were young, or of being an altar boy, they are more open to receive grace now when they are facing death, but they, however, also need the support of prayer.

The family of the dying often do not call the priest, nor do they speak of Heaven nor of God, for fear of upsetting the dying person.

For many, to call a priest to pray with the dying person, or to speak about God is uncomfortable. For some, the situation in which they find themselves leaves them feeling angry at God, and so they distance themselves from Him. There are even those who do not believe in eternal life, or some who believe that they have lived their lives justly, and therefore no forgiveness is necessary.

It may also happen that the priest is not called due to the opinion of others. To some, what the neighbours think seem to be more important than the dying person's need for God's grace. It is also true that a great number of churchgoers do not understand the point of the Sacrament of the Anointing of the Sick. It is not only necessary for eternal salvation, but also for the drastic need of peace with God in the soul of the sick or the dying which is achieved through the Sacraments of Reconciliation and anointing of the sick. They do not understand that this is the sacrament through which God can also heal the most severe illnesses.

God in His mercy is deeply concerned for the conversion and salvation of every human being, but because of His justice and non-bias, He cannot impose His grace on anyone. Prayer for the dying is one of the greatest acts of mercy to which we are all called. No help that we can receive during our lifetime can compare with the help that we will need in the face of our own death.

Simeon saw that a sword would pierce the heart of our Mother Mary, which would reveal the hidden thoughts of many (Luk. 2:35). In doing so, he foretold and revealed a grace by which many of the dying, through her intercession, would recognise and realise the true state in which they lived their lives. In this way, they can see the real motives which were running their deeds, they can ask forgiveness and repent from their heart, thus obtaining salvation. To be able to clearly see one's sinfulness, repent and seek forgiveness – at least before death – is one of the greatest graces which can be given to anyone. None of us are completely aware to what extent we are "in the red" with God. In every *Hail Mary* we ask Jesus and our Mother to constantly *pray for us, sinners*, and especially at the moment of our deaths, so that we can see our sins and at the same time obtain God's mercy. We have to be aware that the Blessed Virgin Mary is present and that she intercedes when we offer Jesus' sacrifice in Mass for the salvation of the dying, precisely because we have uttered those words so often, *"pray for us now and at the hour of our death"*. We need to be aware that she really cares about the eternal life of every dying person, and that at the hour of their death, she is their mother more than ever.

Every dying person can in the last hours of their life store up huge treasures in Heaven if they *heartfully thank God* and their neighbour for all the good which they received during their life. If only they *forgive* others with their whole heart and if they *bless and pray* for all those who are in need of salvation (Mt. 6:19-20). In my opinion, only a few believers really do these things. We should encourage the dying by praying for them to end their lives by storing up treasures for Heaven.

It is not only God who is interested in the dying. The devil is interested as well. Through his servants, he tries to persuade the dying not to seek grace. He accuses them and tries to weigh them down with guilt, and fortifies sentiments of them being rejected by God. The devil tries to pump up their pride in the last hours and convince them that they should not reveal their sinfulness to anyone, especially not to a "sinful priest". The devil will do everything to win over the thoughts and feelings of the dying person so as to divert them away from the road to salvation.

When we offer a Mass for the dying, we should try to offer our own sacrifices too, because we know that sacrifices offered from pure love for a dying person are the most powerful weapons that separate the devil and the dying person.

Offering Mass for the dying is an act that is very close to the heart of God, by which we cooperate with His grace in a special way, but still it is mostly the deep need of the dying person that should primarily motivate us. In the depths of my soul, I know that, in Heaven, we will be brimming with joy when we meet someone whom, even in a tiny way, we helped them to get there.

REDEMPTION FROM SICKNESS

ISAIAH WRITES THAT HE SAW Jesus who, by His sacrifice, accomplished the following for the sick:

- He bore our infirmities and carried our diseases
- He paid the punishment for our sins including those from where sicknesses came or advanced (hatred, bitterness, lack of forgiveness, self-pity, self-accusation, intemperance in food or drink, smoking, drugs, occultism...)
- He healed us by His bruises (Is. 53:4-5).

There are different outcomes of Jesus' redeeming power, and there is always a blessing for the sick. It can take the form of:

- healing
- recognition of the value of suffering
- acceptance of salvation by the remission of sins, acceptance of our passage into eternity.

The Missal contains the rites of the Mass for the Sick which give two options of the collective prayer. In one, we ask God to heal and to restore the sick person to their former health. In the other, we ask for an understanding of the value of suffering. When healing is in question, it is clear what it is about. But often we do not understand the point of another form of redemption: *obtaining recognition of the value of suffering*. We can explain to a sick person the value of suffering if they unite their suffering to that of Jesus' suffering on the cross. With their mind, they can grasp this idea. But understanding alone will not bring acceptance nor inner peace. Acceptance, inner joy and peace come through grace, the grace of understanding and accepting with the heart. This happens when a person understands in his/her heart that the conversion of sinners and other vital graces can be obtained by the offering of our suffering. That recognition is almost always linked to experience.

There are some situations where God knows that it is better for the person to die in a state of grace than to heal. For some, they would return to the old way of life after healing and lose their salvation (especially if their faith is on weak foundations). This is why at the peak experience of faith, the Lord calls them to Himself.

But since the offering of the Mass for the redemption from sickness inevitably leads to thinking about the meaning of life and its value, it can often lead us to a deeper personal conversion and a deeper relationship with God.

It is important to remember that therapy for many illnesses involves the consumption of strong medication which reduces their ability to pray for themselves. This is another reason why praying for the sick, especially offering Masses for their redemption and conversion, is something that every person of faith should have close to their heart.

REDEMPTION FROM PAIN AND FROM WOUNDS OF THE HEART

IN ISAIAH WE READ THAT Jesus took our pains upon Himself. I believe that this primarily refers to the sufferings of the spirit (such as rejection, guilt, low self- esteem, loneliness, bitterness, injustice, etc), and also to any other pain and hurts, including physical pain.

Through the Mass we can gain awareness of the value of pain and suffering, recognise our responsibilities, i.e. the need for repentance and forgiveness towards those who have hurt us, and be freed and healed from pain. The pains of the spirit sometimes extinguish our vital joy and can often negatively affect life, deteriorate health, as well as affect the relationships between spouses, family members, friends, neighbours, etc.

They often cause or significantly contribute to the onset of restlessness, fear, anxieties and various types of psychosis.

During the Holy Mass we can seek our shelter in God, by listening and believing in His holy words and promises: receiving the peace of Jesus, which the world does not know and cannot give, His words, His grace, enter our wounded spirit like an infusion, like the sap that flows from the vine into the branch and gives life. Only God knows us deeply and only He can heal and free us and give us inner peace and happiness. For this reason, also for this intention, a good preparation is extremely important.

LIBERATION FROM SLAVERY TO SIN

SOMETIMES IT HAPPENS THAT EVEN after repeated sincere repentance, penance and confession, we still fall into the same sin. It is possible that we have become enslaved to that sin and in such cases, liberation is needed.

We receive liberation by redemption. We can offer the sacrifice of the Mass for the intention of redemption and liberation from slavery to individual sins for ourselves or others, and especially for our dear ones. Today, it is very easy to become enslaved to: nicotine, alcohol, overeating, drugs, pornography, pedophilia, gambling, betting and other luck-based games "shopaholicism", gossiping, false accusations and judgementalism, credulity, lewdness and uttering obscenities, cursing, the Internet, television, gaming, and all types of dependencies, attachments and bondage.

These problems often wreak havoc on our spiritual, psychological and physical health, destroying marriages and families, and drag us before eternal judgement. Many of those problems have their roots in difficult life circumstances which we lived through in our earliest childhood, after which we felt rejected, unwanted, less worthy or guilty. For this reason, it is very important to have a proper preparation for the Mass, which will dispose our hearts to receive the graces of inner healing, forgiveness, and liberation. Sometimes we will have to offer more than only one Mass for that intention (especially if the root of the problem lies in deep wounds of the soul), conscious that our God is dealing little by little, and will liberate us and lead us gradually into His peace.

(CCC 1363; Rom. 6:16-17; Rom. 7:14-25)

FOR SOMEONE'S CONVERSION

EVERYONE NEEDS CONVERSION. THE FIRST conversion happens when our heart decides for God and the second is *ongoing* and through it, we, by the grace of God, try to become better and better.

When we pray for this and offer Jesus' sacrifice to the Father, we can be sure that we are asking for something that is absolutely in harmony with the will of God.

God will not force anyone to convert, but He can draw whoever we are praying for very close to Himself, into His love. That "attracting" depends greatly on the strength of our desire for their conversion. It depends on how much we love. That love bursts out and is transformed into attracting in the moments when we pray, when we offer the Holy Mass, and when we freely offer sacrifices for them.

Masses, for that initial conversion, should be offered until we feel our prayer has been answered. Sometimes the fruits are immediately seen, sometimes we have to wait a while. Sometimes that initial conversion will only take place on their deathbed. God in His providence and His love knows when it is best for them.

When we see that the initial conversion, that fundamental decision has been made, we should continue to pray, to offer Masses for the second *ongoing* conversion, in whatever way the Spirit leads.

This is especially important for parents in latter years, who have enough wisdom to understand what is most lacking in their children, who in the meantime have become parents themselves.

RECEIVING BLESSINGS IN OUR LIFE CALLING

MASSES ARE NECESSARY FOR THE realisation of our life's calling too, and especially for our life mission. Sometimes on the road to the realisation of life mission, there is a blockage, which we by ourselves cannot be liberated from. That is why it is very important to offer Masses to redeem us from everything that is stopping us or obstructing us from realising our mission in life. To be a good priest, a good religious, a good spouse, a good father, a good mother, son, daughter, friend, to be a good person in one's life's work, career or profession, is impossible without God's grace. Only grace can effectively free us, form us, encourage us, raise us up, direct us, protect us, strengthen and heal us...

REMISSION FOR DAMAGES

SIN IS AN INJUSTICE WHICH will always cause damages, either to ourselves or to others. For example, if we cause financial harm to someone, and afterwards we wish to make amends, one of the ways to do so is by offering that same amount of money back to that person. But how can we make up for the disappointment, the pain, sorrow and mistrust that we have caused (theft, deception, blackmail, lack of concern...)? The good news is that there is no damage that we can do with our sins that God Almighty cannot redeem. In other words, God can turn to good all the evil we do to others into the very blessings for them. By our sincere offering of the Mass for the redemption of the effects which befell someone because of our sins, God can take the pain that we caused to others and ourselves. God can grant the grace to repair their hearts, the grace for those whom we have hurt can find peace in their souls again, the grace to restore a relationship of trust with us, the grace to forgive. God can even give that person compensation in another *currency*. In other words, He can give them something that is more necessary for their soul. Whatever we seek with faith for those against whom we have sinned, it will be granted (Mk. 11: 24; Jn. 14:13; Jn. 15:7; Jn. 16:23).

Sometimes we will not be able to find peace up until - with our penance, our prayers, our Mass offerings and our own sacrifice - grace is received in the souls of those whom we have sinned against.

It is desirable that after serious sin, such as abortion, we offer a Mass for someone who is in a similar temptation, or who will be in that situation in the future. In this way, we can help them to overcome that temptation or that if they have succumbed to temptation, they will be able to find peace in true contrition and confession. Deeds done for the purpose of reparation for wrongs is a symptom of true contrition, an expression of true love of God and our neighbour, and is often the best way to atone for the sin committed. These deeds bring us into the reality of the ugliness of sin and act as a protection against falling into that sin again.

It is good then to repair the damage that was done and to offer our own sacrifices. For example, in the case of abortion, we can offer to educate a child in Africa through missionary funds.

RECEIVING MATERIAL BLESSINGS

OUR HEAVENLY FATHER CARES FOR us and wishes that in everything we have enough and that we live with dignity. He even wishes those who abound in material and financial goods that they share them with those who are in even greater need (2 Cor. 9:8). People who know Jesus from the Gospel know that the goods that they are sharing are not their own, but that rather God Himself entrusted the goods to them. Those people know that they did not get those goods, regardless of how hard they worked, to keep them only for themselves and spend them for their own pleasures, but rather to bless those around them in need.

The fruit of offering Masses for material blessings is often a change of heart, giving us an increased consciousness in managing the blessings bestowed on us.

Sometimes we do not receive the material blessing, because, as the apostle James tells us (Jas. 4:3), we would only spend the money on inordinate desires. Some of the worst inordinate desires are: *the desire to possess, the desire to dominate, the desire for control and power.*

Sometimes the reasons for long-lasting and insoluble material and financial problems, can be interior decisions, inner vows that we uttered to our own detriment. I have personal experience of how true this is.

In my early childhood, I was humiliated because of my family's poverty, so that, at one moment, I decided deep within myself that I did not want to become rich – with my own will I firmly decided that I wanted to be poor in order to avoid further disappointment. Some people have determined their whole lives in this way and will not be able to enjoy financial blessing until Jesus liberates them from their own deep inner decisions.

Some have, for example, made similar inner decisions: *I will never marry, I will never have children*. They have forgotten this, but their inner decision is still active and stops them from receiving blessings. Others, again, have decided that they will do everything they can in order to be rich one day and, because of that, they cannot stop accumulating riches unless God's grace liberates them.

Blessings can also be blocked with negative attitudes and negative words from people who had authority over us in our childhood; for example, our parents, a teacher, a priest... Many are still under the influence of rash words such as: "You will never succeed at anything! You will always be hungry! You are totally incapable of earning!"

Sometimes we are only enslaved by fears, feelings of guilt or feelings of inferiority...

Jesus can and will redeem us of all of these things. I repeat, He wants us to have enough of everything, and even more. He wants us to give, to help those who are in need, and it is necessary to help them in order to live with dignity.

OBTAINING BLESSINGS FOR OUR INTERPERSONAL RELATIONSHIPS

PEOPLE CAN BE ENSLAVED IN many different ways. For example, in the breakdown of interpersonal relationships in marriage, in the family, in the workplace. Many circumstances can lead to a situation where two or more people can no longer speak to each other, or do not understand each other, nor accept each other, and they judge each other and live in fear of each other. Redemption in these situations could take place as a process of dwelling in God's redeeming love. Dwelling in God, in the grace of His peace, heals wounds and enables us to forgive. It helps us to see why we behave in this way, so that we can pray with faith in our heart and so that we can accept our neighbour, love him as he or she is, and that we can experience God's protection. Also, dwelling in God enables us to see the attachments which harm us and from which we must escape. Sometimes we are so attached to another person, or that person is so attached to us, that we must seek redemption and liberation from that relationship.

SPIRITUAL STRENGTH

AT THE BEGINNING OF THE Holy Mass, in the Act of Contrition, or repentance, we recognise our sins and our sinful tendencies with which we are in constant battle. Sometimes we even lose that battle. We admit our lack of willpower : we do too little good, we sacrifice ourselves too little, and we spend too little time with and in God. We recognise that the degree of love we have towards our neighbour is way below what it should be and what we would like to present to God. We accept that we need God's wisdom in order to make wise decisions. For this reason, we come to Mass for the grace of Jesus to surpass the influence of the flesh and the world upon us.

LIBERATION AND PROTECTION FROM DEMONIC INFLUENCE

WE KNOW THAT THERE ARE people who practice various types of occult works with the aim of damaging others. We need to know though that, it is difficult to do damage to someone who has already built up resistance by their close relationship to God and who is used to spiritual warfare (Eph. 6:10-20).

Resorting to the occult does damage at all different levels. In fact, the biggest problems occur when people go looking for help in the wrong places. These people almost always fall into the trap that the devil wanted all along: judging, bitterness, and even hatred, to the point of corroding the essence of their very soul.

When we offer the Holy Mass for the redemption from demonic influences, it is important to know that the process that is most necessary, is forgiving from our heart those who have sinned or still sin against us, that we bless them and that we pray for them, and that we do not seek to know who cursed us or caused us problems unless we are capable of loving our enemies.

It is also important to know that the reason why we were so easily attacked or defeated is because we did not have a strong enough relationship with God. It is important to recognise this and confess it and to decide to spend time building up our relationship with God. If we do not build up this relationship, then the liberation which we receive from this redemption will not be long-lived, or we will not be able to gain it in the first place.

Therefore, it is important to prepare for the offering of the Mass. Without it, we cannot arrive at what we are seeking.

GROWTH IN THE FRUITS OF THE HOLY SPIRIT

By offering the intentions of the Mass for ourselves or for others, through the intensive dwelling within God's grace, God rebuilds us more and more in His likeness, in perfection of the fruits of the Spirit: love, joy, peace, patience, kindness, generosity, faithfulness, gentleness, and self-control (Gal. 5:22). That continuous growth in the fruits of the Spirit, brings about a continuous change of heart, conversion and consecration and it must become a motivation for active and fruitful participation in the Holy Mass. A qualitative change of heart is something that always delights the Lord, but it should also delight those with whom we live and, most of all, it should gladden our own hearts.

THE HOLY MASS AND GOD'S WORD

Almighty God, grant that we may listen and obey the promptings of Your Spirit: that we may hear Your voice and with our words and our lives follow You. Through our Lord.

(Collective prayer)

BESIDES COMING TO US THROUGH the Body and Blood of His Son, God also comes to us at the Mass in His Word when the readings are proclaimed. We all know how the words of someone who is important to us mean; words of support, of comfort, of encouragement, of warning, words of respect, of recognition, love, acceptance, praise, advice... Who would not want to hear those words from God, especially if we find ourselves in difficult life situations?!

Sometimes, God's Word is the only medicine, the only comfort. In many situations in life, He is the only one who can bring hope, peace, and healing (Ps. 107:20). Sometimes, His counsel is the only thing that will help us make the right decision. Through the Word of God, all things were created, and that same Word can recreate, renew, heal, and set free...

The hearing of the Word of God from the Sacred Scriptures in the celebration of the Mass is of utmost importance. The Holy Spirit first recalls the meaning of the salvation event to the liturgical assembly by giving life to the Word of God, which is proclaimed so that it may be received and lived. From the Sacred Scriptures come the lessons that are read and explained in the homily and the psalms that are sung. It is from the Scriptures that the prayers, collects, and hymns draw their inspiration (CCC 1100).

Jesus is the incarnate Word of God and so, when we receive the Word, we receive Him (Jn. 1:1-15). When we know the Word, we know the heart of God (CCC 112). This is why when the Word is received in the heart, it can bring supernatural changes in the spirit, the soul, and the body.

At the Mass, God speaks to our understanding, but also to our inner person.

It is important that, when we go to Mass, we go with the conviction that everyone of us is important to God, that He sees our needs and that He wishes to speak to each of us personally. I would repeat the following: God created all of us so that we could live forever. He put us in this world so that we could determine our eternal fate during our short time here. For that reason, every moment of our life is important for Him. That is why He is ready to get involved in every situation in life to which we will call Him, and He is always ready to speak to each of us personally.

Can He comfort us, encourage us, warn us, teach us, lead us if He cannot speak to us?

At every Holy Mass, the Sower, God, sows His Word so that in our lives it would bring forth manifold fruits (CCC 1101). This is why we should have this parable written in our hearts.

> *When a great crowd gathered and people from town after town came to him, he said in a parable: "A sower went out to sow his seed; and as he sowed, some fell on the path and was trampled on, and the birds of the air ate it up. Some fell on the rock; and as it grew up, it withered for lack of moisture. Some fell among thorns, and the thorns grew with it and choked it. Some fell into good soil, and when it grew, it produced a hundredfold." As he said this, he called out, "Let anyone with ears to hear listen!"*
>
> *"Now the parable is this: The seed is the word of God. The ones on the path are those who have heard; then the devil comes and takes away the word from their hearts, so that they may not believe and be saved. The ones on the rock are those who, when they hear the word, receive it with joy. But these have no root; they believe only for a while and in a time of testing fall away. As for what fell among the thorns, these are the ones who hear; but as they go on their way, they are choked by the cares and riches and pleasures of life, and their fruit does not mature. But as for that in the good soil, these are the ones who, when they hear the word, hold it fast in an honest and good heart, and bear fruit with patient endurance."*
>
> *(Lk. 8:4-8, 11-15; Mt. 13:1-9; Mk. 4:1-9)*

Many times, we have heard the Word and *received it with joy*. It touched us in a special way, it touched us significantly. These were words which we began to ponder, which fired up our imagination, desire, and emotions

(CCC 2708). Many of those words encouraged us to cooperate with God's grace in a special way for our temporal and eternal benefit. But too often we did not persevere in this. We did not manage to *conserve* the Word, to *hold it in our hearts* and it did not bear fruit in our life.

God longs for this, to speak to us personally, because He knows how much we need His Word, how much power those words have when they enter into our heart and are cherished in it. Jesus wishes explicitly that we love Him so much that we receive and cherish His Word in our hearts and that we learn to live from that Word (Jn. 14:23-24; Mt. 4:4). God's word, cherished in the heart, opens up a space for the Spirit to act. It develops His fruits and gifts within us so that we become a blessing to ourselves and others.

There is no situation in life which God's almighty Word cannot turn into a blessing.

At every Holy Mass, we hear many holy words that are taken from the Sacred Scripture or inspired by it. All of them can become a true blessing to one *who cherishes them in his/her hearts*.

If we wish to hear (discern) the Word which God has intended for us, with which he wishes to touch us in a special way, we should not expect a thunderous voice, or strong talk accompanied by very emotional or touching sentiments, even though it can even come in that way. Let us learn to listen in the peace and silence of our hearts, completely concentrated on the words which we are listening to or speaking. Let our hearts be like the peaceful surface of the water, on which we can notice even a gentle breeze. Just as the quality of a plant is not based on the noise of the seed as it falls on the ground, in the same way, the importance of the Word of God should not be compared with the intensity with which we experience it. I have learnt that the Word which is barely noticeable when it enters the heart often has greater worth than that which enters in a dramatic way.

We must live from every word that comes from the mouth of God, we must long for the words which are directed to us personally, not with anxious expectations, but rather with peaceful surrendering, with trust that God will speak at the right time and in the right way.

A part of the necessary preparation for the Holy Mass is the entrance into the presence of God. To do this we must silence our heart, calm our feelings (whether positive or negative), and keep our attention on what is happening in the liturgy.

When we focus our attention on God, our will, thoughts and feelings are appeased and we can *taste and enjoy the Word.*

How does God speak to us personally? Here are some of the ways:

THE ROLE OF THE PRIEST

THE PRIEST REPRESENTS CHRIST. HE is actually *Alter Christus and Persona Christi.* He presents to the Lord all our prayers and petitions, he offers the Mass sacrifice on behalf of the Church and the parish community, he pronounces Christ's words at the transubstantiation. Through him, God blesses us and speaks to us.

For the parishioners, it is beautiful and very useful when the priest is in love with the liturgy, when he lives from the Mass. How beautiful and useful it is for the parishioners when the priest is in love with God's Word, when he is experienced in meditation and his life is an expression of a life built on the Word of God. When a priest is constantly building on his intimate relationship with God, and heartily intercedes for the flock that has been entrusted to him, when it is clear to the congregation that their priest has personal experience of the closeness of God, then there is a contagious quality about his behaviour.

How beautiful it is when the priest has this contagious effect on his flock. When he has the experience of the Mass in his heart, to the extent that he lives it and speaks of it in a way that draws others.

The same can be said about his attitude to the Sacred Scripture, to prayer, to sacrifice... If the priest himself has a personal experience of the Scriptures, prayer, sacrifice, of offering his suffering, then he is capable of speaking about it in a way that draws others.

So, this *infectiousness* should ideally start with the priest, and from him should spread to the church and from them to all people of good will. This infectiousness is in its essence evangelization.

One of the primary tasks of the priest is to motivate the faithful to understand, taste, and love the Mass. When priests testify from their own experience about the participation in the Mass, the faithful understand them and are ready to follow them in this experience.

No priest is capable of doing this if he is not used to it, if he has not learned to spend time with God, filling himself with God's grace, if he has not learned to remain in Him, if he has not grown in grace and wisdom before God and his brethren.

The Church teaches us to meditate on God's Word from our earliest days in order to live from it. A priest who is in love with the Word of God and experienced in its meditation will easily communicate to his congregation this love towards the Word of God and the possibility to meditate.

I can thank God that I had these types of priests in my earliest youth. Their love of Jesus in the Eucharist had such an effect on me that I often came alone to the church to adore Jesus, especially through the Eucharistic songs: *Jesus, we adore You. O Sacrament most Holy. Holy God, we praise Thy name.* I thank God that I had a catechist who was in love with the Word of God, with the Bible, and who spoke to us about various biblical books so that we all listened to him willingly. I thank God for my parents who communicated a great love towards the Blessed Virgin, the saints, and the souls in purgatory, because they "infected" me with faith through their powerful intercession. I am grateful to them because they bought magazines and books that were in the spirit of the Church, that inspired love for God, the Church, and service.

I would not like to be misunderstood, but I have noticed that in some countries, and in some regions, and even in some of our parishes, much fewer children go to Mass than when I was young. I think that the reason for this is that they have teachers (whether priests or lay persons) who have knowledge, but they lack enthusiasm or passion in their ministry.

However, of one thing I am sure: there is no priest or catechist in that work whom God Himself did not call, and it is never too late to go back to our first love – God, and ask Him to ignite us again if we seek Him with all of our hearts. If this is something that we really want, our years, our experience or even spiritual dryness can stop. I am also convinced that every believer can find God if they seek Him with all of their hearts.

It is the duty of all of us to pray and offer sacrifices for our priests and catechists of our children, because God can do a lot of good through a priest or catechist who is loved, respected, and is strongly supported by the prayers of the community.

I wish to emphasise that by baptism we all share in the priesthood of Jesus' sacrifice to the Father. Only an ordained priest can utter the words of the consecration, but everyone of the faithful can, by their priestly privilege received at baptism offer Jesus' sacrifice for their own redemption or for the redemption of others. We can also offer our own sacrifices. We should be grateful that we can participate in Jesus' redemptive sacrifice, so that we can, in this way, both receive and intercede for others' for spiritual and temporal welfare.

I know from experience that this sort of thinking cannot be accepted in a man's heart until we have had a taste of it.

THE WORD ECHOES IN OUR HEARTS

CCC 2688: "*The catechesis of children, young people, and adults aims at teaching them to meditate on The Word of God in personal prayer, practicing it in liturgical prayer, and internalizing it at all times in order to bear fruit in a new life. Catechesis is also a time for the discernment and education of popular piety. The memorization of basic prayers offers an essential support to the life of prayer, but it is important to help learners savor their meaning.*"

The Spirit makes some words "stand out" so that they take our attention in a particular way and that we discern them separately from the rest (CCC 2706). We can recognize which ones they are because they provoke deeper thought, imagination, emotion, and desire (CCC 2708).

Even though we perhaps hear the same words over and over again, - *words of comfort, support, corrections and warnings* -(that come to us through listening the Scripture readings at Mass), there will come a time when we hear them in a *different way,* and at that point they become part of us. From these words, we can draw constant counsel and blessing. These words are different precisely because they touched us. They take on a concrete meaning in certain situations, and that meaning provokes us to think deeply, and to recognize the intended good and blessing which they represent. They spark certain imaginations and emotions in us and give us a desire to direct our lives toward them (CCC 2708).

Unfortunately, in our lives we have heard many negative words too, which, if we reacted in the same way, probably did a lot of damage to us.

I once found myself in a business situation which could have ended badly for me. I went to the morning Mass and placed that situation in the hands of God. Focused and in peace I listened, expecting God to speak to me. I awaited the confirmation that God had heard my prayer. But all the words were of equal importance to me. Right up until the end of the Mass, completely unexpectedly the words of the priest "Go in peace" touched me deeply (every Mass in Croatia ends with these words). In that instant, I knew that God had heard my prayer and that everything would be well. I thanked Him, and, in fact, everything did go well.

At one moment, I became blocked while correcting this book, and I could not go forward with it. Then, during the offertory prayers during the morning Mass, the words rang within me: *"Grant, Lord, that we may always thank You in this eternal mystery. Through it, You continuously correct us: may it be a continual fountain of eternal joy. Through Christ".* At that moment, I knew that I would continue with my writing without further blocks. And that is how it was. After Mass, I returned home and sat at my computer.

It is especially at the Holy Mass, that I hear *in a special way* , words which answer a question that is in my heart. The questions are the result of meditating on God, His word and life, and are a further motivation to listen carefully for God's *answers.* The words I hear, often open up new questions about things that I have never even thought about, but they, in turn, open up new dimensions in my connection with God.

At the Holy Mass, I listen in the same way to words which advise me, raise me up, comfort me, and direct my paths.

Even while working on this book, the Lord has led me through many Masses and showed me the way.

GOD INSPIRES THE PRIESTS

SC 11: "But in order that the liturgy may be able to produce its full effects, it is necessary that the faithful come to it with proper dispositions, that their minds should be attuned to their voices, and that they should cooperate with divine grace lest they receive it in vain. Pastors of souls must therefore realize that, when the liturgy is celebrated, something more is required than the mere observation of the laws governing valid and licit celebration; it is their duty also to ensure that the faithful take part fully aware of what they are doing, actively engaged in the rite, and enriched by its effects."

MANY CHURCHGOERS WILL TESTIFY TO the fact that sometimes at the Holy Mass they heard exactly the answer to the question they had about their situation in life in a way that they could understand and accept. To many of us, it seemed as if the priest said those words differently and they touched us so deeply because he stressed them in a particular way. God wanted our hearts to be moved in this way.

It happened many times that things that the priest mentioned in a particular way gave me a strengthened conviction in that regard. It made my faith stronger. Many times, I learned something new about God or the Church. Many times, I was led to later contemplating something that the priest had talked about in his homily.

The sermon is something that I have always listened to since I was very young. I am always happy when something that I have learned can be applied to my everyday life, thanks to so many priests who give themselves with love, and share their knowledge and experience to the faithful; many lay people also feel encouraged to bring these lessons to those who have less knowledge or experience in the faith.

GOD SPEAKS DIRECTLY TO US

CCC 2706: *"To meditate on what we read helps us to make it our own by confronting it with ourselves. Here, another book is opened: the book of life. We pass from thoughts to reality. To the extent that we are humble and faithful, we discover in meditation the movements that stir the heart and we are able to discern them. It is a question of acting truthfully in order to come into the light: "Lord, what do you want me to do?"*

THROUGH HIS SPIRIT, GOD CAN sometimes speak in a way that is clearly heard in our hearts. It happens rarely which is why we remember those words, we meditate more on those words, and we hardly ever forget them.

At the beginning of my service as an evangelist, I found myself in a difficult situation. As I was praying for a situation, God spoke some words to me that I knew were written somewhere in the Scriptures. I opened my Bible and found them at once. They were words from the Book of Revelation:

"I know your works. Look, I have set before you an open door, which no one is able to shut. I know that you have but little power, and yet you have kept my word and have not denied my name" (Rev. 3:8).

Those holy words have brought multiple fruits into my life. Many times they have opened a door for me in a miraculous way, and brought peace and joy to my heart. Since then I pay special attention and give weight to those words. In so many ways, they have directed my pathway to eternity.

Another such example happened to a friend of mine whose beloved wife died of cancer. After the funeral, he came to the church to the Requiem Mass. While collecting himself in preparation for the Mass, he clearly heard the words: "Come to me, all you that are weary and are carrying heavy burdens, and I will give you rest" (Mt. 11:28). He raised his eyes to the altar and he saw the same words written on the altar image. At once, he was filled with inner peace and joy. That peace and joy remained in his heart for days. In his whole being, he knew that his wife was saved.

GOD GIVES DISCERNMENT

CCC 1101: *"The Holy Spirit gives a spiritual understanding of the Word of God to those who read or hear it, according to the dispositions of their hearts. By means of the words, actions, and symbols that form the structure of a celebration, the Spirit puts both the faithful and the ministers into a living relationship with Christ, the Word and Image of the Father, so that they can live out the meaning of what they hear, contemplate, and do in the celebration."*

SOMETIMES, DURING THE MASS, GOD gives us an insight, even though we might not be aware of it and we only become aware of it after the Mass.

It might happen that, after the Mass, we have the impression that something we are praying for will be answered, even though during the Mass we received no such sign, nor did we hear or experience anything in particular.

Sometimes we simply know that that day or very soon afterwards something very significant is going to happen. Sometimes, after the Mass, we are prompted to do something very concrete. Perhaps we are prompted to go and visit someone or that we pray or fast for someone or that we go somewhere. Or we simply know that there is something we are not supposed to do, something we are to avoid, or that we have to repent of something.

This is the result of Jesus' Eucharistic presence within us , who is whispering to our inner selves.

GOD REMINDS US

THE SPIRIT OFTEN PROMPTS US at Mass when we are reminded of certain people or situations in life. Various people come to our minds that we were not even thinking of. We may have not seen them for years nor have we been thinking of them. It could be someone that we only know, but do not know their name.

Very often the Spirit reminds me of someone who died. By praying for the souls in purgatory and offering the Mass for them, I can clearly see that I am growing in love towards God and people close to me. I am certain that my growth is a response to their prayers for me to thank me for my intercession. Because who knows better than the souls in purgatory what we need most in this earthly life?!

Often, especially during the presentation of the gifts, people who are either near death or who have wandered far off the path of the Lord come to my mind. We must be aware that God has entrusted them to our prayers. Otherwise, He would not have inspired us to pray for these people.

God can remind us of people or situations so that, by thinking about them, we will draw a conclusion or it inspires an idea in us. Sometimes that *reminding* is just a switch which will activate our imagination, feelings and will towards something that the Spirit is asking of us.

God also reminds us of the sins that we have committed and never repented for, or of people we have not forgiven, or of someone against whom we are holding a grudge, or of promises or vows that we have not kept.

This reminding, when it comes from the Spirit, does not upset our following of the Mass in any way, but rather brings us deeper into the presence of God.

GOD PROMPTS US IN VISIONS

CCC 2707: *"There are as many and varied methods of meditation as there are spiritual masters. Christians owe it to themselves to develop the desire to meditate regularly, lest they come to resemble the three first kinds of soil in the parable of the sower. But a method is only a guide; the important thing is to advance, with the Holy Spirit, along the one way of prayer: Christ Jesus."*

VISIONS CAN ALSO HELP IN the active and fruitful participation in the Mass.

A married couple who are dear friends of mine participated in the Mass in which their son received the Sacrament of Confirmation. During the presentation of the gifts, the mother had a vision of Jesus who was coming towards her with a young man who seemed slightly older than her son who had been confirmed. Jesus and the young man smiled at her. The young man was vaguely familiar to her, but she could not remember where she knew him from. As he drew very close to her, the young man whispered: "Mommy". At that moment, the vision disappeared, and she recognised her first son whom she had lost in a miscarriage, which she had never really gotten over, up until that moment. When she told her husband what had happened to her, both of them cried, deeply moved. God had, during this Holy Mass and in this miraculous way, healed their deep wound.

A vision during Mass can last only a couple of seconds, but in it we can see our whole lives pass by in small details. In God's visions, there are no limits on time and space. If it happens during the liturgy, it does not disturb our participation in the Mass. On the contrary, it leads us deeper into the mystery of the Eucharist.

I remember how, as a boy, during the Mass, I would have visions of saints and angels. I did not give it much attention, because I thought everyone else could see them too. I can definitely say that what I saw with open eyes was not the fruit of my imagination, because at that time I neither thought about nor expected them.

Recently, I have realised that in my heart I judge certain people, that I mention them too often in a negative way and that Jesus is not pleased about this. I offered the Mass that God would forgive me for this and that He would give me a new heart for these people. During the elevation, I had a vision of some of them in Heaven in a higher position than my own, with a greater dignity. Looking at them, I felt great joy because of them. There was no trace of jealousy or envy in me. What is more, I was filled with joy and respect towards them. I clearly realised that in Heaven everyone knows that his place is completely justly decided and for this reason nobody feels envy. That short vision did a lot of good for my spiritual growth and, in the end, changed my attitude towards those people. During the vision, I clearly knew that I was in Heaven, but I was aware of only the piece of what was necessary in order to answer the intention for which I had offered the Mass.

We can have a vision with open or with closed eyes. We can have so wonderful visions that we get the impression that we are in a different dimension, outside the body and outside the world, or our visions can be so vague as if they are masked by fog. What is worthwhile, for listening to the Word of God, holds true here too: the intensity of the vision does not necessarily have to be in the same measure as its importance.

HOW CAN WE BE SURE THAT IT IS GOD WHO IS SPEAKING TO US?

How can we know if what we are seeing or hearing is coming from God and not from our own spirit, or worse, from the devil? Here are some of the criteria:

One of the basic criterion is that it does not disturb us, but rather, on the contrary, it brings us even closer to what is happening in the Mass.

Another criterion is generally doubt. That is, God's Word often brings certain changes to the way we are thinking or new information which we did not possess until then. It is completely normal then, for our subconsciousness to revolt slightly and doubt its content. In this case, doubt is just a warning to our subconsciousness that what we have heard or experienced is different to what we have heard or experienced up until then, which is why when we think that God has spoken to us, it is always better to wait to see if we will react with doubt. That doubt can be an added assurance that our experience or the message or information received was not from our own subconsciousness. Sometimes the doubt is very strong, and from experience we can even discern that it comes from the evil one who wants to persuade us into not believing and accepting it. This can assure us even more that the very experience comes from God because God inspires, He does not impose.

Furthermore, God will never reveal something that is contrary to His Word. He neither judges nor accuses. He will warn us, but He does not humiliate nor hurt. Nor does He use force.

Plus, and this is very important to know, God is ready to say the same thing to us over and over again, up until we are able to listen to it and accept it.

Another sure way of recognising the source of the words or recognition or experience, is if the fruits of that experience are the fruits of the Spirit which are listed in the _Epistle to the Ephesians_. That is, if they result in positive changes in our heart, then we can be pretty sure that it is God who is speaking (Eph. 5:22).

The ability to discern becomes deeper with experience. God knows our spiritual capacity. He wishes us to discern and to try things out. This is why He gives us certain "Words" and experiences taking into account that we will need more time and maybe a deeper inspiration in order to recognise and accept.

When God speaks within us, the words come with gratefulness and we are stimulated to glorify God and bless Him. This creates a longing within us to read and investigate the Scriptures, a desire to get to know Him even better, to spend more time with Him alone. If someone thinks that God is speaking to Him during the Mass, and this does not lead one to reading and meditating on the Scriptures, especially if it is accompanied by a strong desire to communicate this message to others, we can be pretty sure that it is not God speaking.

If we suffer from psychological conditions, we need to be very careful. In that case, it is not good to give much attention to supernatural messages because our subconsciousness is overactive, and much of what we see and hear in a heightened way does not come from God, but from our own subconsciousness.

HOW TO ATTAIN A BETTER UNDERSTANDING

Lord, grant that we approach these sacraments with due respect.
Whenever we celebrate the memory of Christ's sacrifice, the work
of redemption is completed within us. Through Christ.

(Offertory prayer)

TODAY, WE CAN FIND MANY high-quality sources which speak about the order of the Holy Mass: missalettes, prayer books, parish newsletters, internet pages which touch upon the themes of the faithful etc. We can also find quite a number of texts about priesthood and the role of priests at the Mass. That is why I decided to deal with only the observations closely linked with the theme of the book itself. These observations are the fruit of my own meditation and experiences, or the fruit of the meditations of those who work on the liturgy and whose lectures I had the pleasure of reading or listening to.

SILENCE IS GOLDEN

I AM WRITING THIS FOR priests.

It is extremely important to leave enough silence after words are uttered so that those who are listening can understand and accept them in their hearts, and then become conscious enough to accompany the uttered prayers with their own invocations (spoken thoughts or expressions to unify ourselves with the act). It is enough to leave a few seconds after each utterance. A little more time would be necessary after each reading so that those attending the Mass can consolidate in their minds what they considered important in the reading and to be able to ponder in their heart (Jn. 14:23-24). In the majority of cases, a minute after the reading would be enough. However, the most important thing is to leave a few minutes after Communion. In some churches, I have been pleasantly surprised by the silence that lasted a few minutes afterwards. On Sundays and feast days in those churches, the choir sings until Holy Communion has been distributed. Afterwards there is complete silence for a few moments. At this time, the most important part of the Mass takes place. I am under the impression that the laity are completely aware of the importance of that silence and that they are grateful for it. Saint John Paul II often stressed that he was living from those few minutes of silence during which he was able to immerse himself in God. The same goes for many other saints, and many of the faithful who had or have the privilege of tasting in silence a true encounter with their

Saviour and Redeemer. Those few minutes are crucial for active and effective participation in the Mass.

Here, I would just like to emphasise, as I often do, that Holy Masses are completely valid, even when they are not celebrated according to specific intentions , or when they are not adequately prepared for, or when they are offered by priests who are lacking in enthusiasm, and when they do not have sufficient pauses or when they do not try to ease the participation of the faithful and the disposition of their hearts. Even in those Masses, Christ gives Himself completely. But the fruitfulness of the Mass is greatly influenced by the disposition of the hearts of those attending, and that disposition is affected by the aforementioned.

There is one more thing that I would like to add. Sometimes it is possible to say a few words about the person for whom we are offering the Mass. When this is done, it disposes the hearts of the faithful to care more and invest themselves more in praying for the intention or for the deceased.

THE PEACE THAT THE WORLD CANNOT GIVE

PEACE IS ONE OF THE most often mentioned and most important words in the Bible and in the liturgy. Peace is the fruit of the Holy Spirit, the fruit of His action in our hearts, the fruit of grace, of mercy, the fruit of dwelling in God's presence.

In the Mass, we pray for the peace of Christ, which surpasses any peace that comes from this world. He Himself is our peace. In order to understand the peace of Christ, we have to ask what is the opposite of peace? Maybe we could describe it with the following: fear, anxiety, guilt, woundedness, disappointment, pain, hatred, unforgiveness, bitterness, helplessness, unwantedness, rejection, insecurity, indecisiveness, mistrust, jealousy, envy, worry for our family...

All of these states of the soul and spirit rob us of peace. Many of us know how to bury this "unpeace" into our subconscious mind! But, at times, it is no longer possible to suppress it and then it comes to the surface and creates many problems.

The unrest can also be the fruit of the Holy Spirit. The Holy Spirit can sometimes disturb our heart to convict us and show us the need of God's mercy. The Holy Spirit can waken up our consciousness so that we are inspired to sacrifice ourselves for others or do good for them.

The only real solution for the problem of unrest and lack of peace as Jesus gives it is redemption by surrendering everything to the will of God. That is what this book is about.

Beginning with the introductory greeting at the Mass (the second or third line, the bishop's greeting) and even throughout the Mass, but especially at the Communion rite, we pray for the peace of Christ. We ask Him to give us His peace in our day (and not just when we get to paradise): that we are free from all anxiety which sin has brought into our hearts, our lives and our families, so that we are free from the evil one.

The peak of the Mass is partaking of the Lamb, the Lamb of God whom we directly ask before Communion to give us His peace. Jesus, entering us through Communion pronounces that peace to our soul in the same way He did when He entered into any house in the Gospels, just as He did with His disciples when He sent them out two by two (Mt. 10:12-13; Lk. 10:5-6).

When we are in danger and we cannot see the way out, His peace gives us a certainty that He is with us, and that there is no need for our hearts to be anxious. Whatever bad can happen, we have to believe that the peace of Jesus is at our disposition. Let us remember that all things work together for good for those who love Him. Christ's peace is also a powerful proof that God has answered our prayer.

There are situations in life from which God cannot free us. For example, He cannot free us from the obligation to care for a child who is mentally ill, but He can give us His peace so that we know that He is with us and that whatever we are doing has its significance in eternity.

At Mass, we come to receive the peace of Christ in order to cherish it and offer it to others.

THE ENCOUNTER WITH THE LIVING GOD

RECEIVING HOLY COMMUNION IS THE climax for us at Mass. God wanted that in it, through it and with it, by becoming one with Jesus, we become partakers in His divine nature. When we receive Holy Communion, Jesus with His flesh, blood, humanity and divinity enters us and remains for as long as the particles subsist in us (CCC 1374).

The depth of that meeting inside me, a believer with the sacrificed Jesus, depends to a great extent on the disposition of my own heart. The whole Mass up until that point is directed towards my arriving at this summit point. That is why we could divide the Mass spiritually into two parts: preparation for Communion and Communion itself. After receiving Communion, I enter into my inner being in order to meet and experience Jesus. In other words, I direct my spiritual and physical attention on the presence of Jesus within me by glorifying Him, blessing Him and thanking Him, handing over whatever is in my heart and continuing with my inner prayer.

When I am in Him, I am filled with the Holy Spirit, I am filled with a love that is poured out from the Father, and I am enabled to surrender myself to the Father's will. When I am in Him, I am ready (I really wish with my whole heart), and I am enabled (by the grace of the Holy Spirit) to forgive my greatest enemies. In Him, I can hand over those wounds that cause me the greatest pain and receive inner healing and release from their bondage. Together with Him, with faith in my heart, I can pray to the Father for others and sincerely bless and thank Him with my whole being as the Holy Spirit guides me to.

Sometimes Eucharistic Communion can turn into a mystical experience of the love of God and His presence, and sometimes God wants us just to have faith, which is the case when my outer person does not experience anything in particular.

At any rate, even the slightest experience will increase my nearness to God. By experience, I mean the slightest touch of grace by which my consciousness is heightened in any way. We all know that Jesus said that those who believe and do not see are more blessed. He said this after the apostle Thomas had to put his fingers into the wounds in order to believe. It was said to the apostles when He appeared to them and reprimanded them for their hardness of heart and lack of belief. We should ask ourselves this question: "Do I have this kind of belief that I do not need proof?" If we have, then its fruits are clearly visible in our lives. If we do not, we know what Jesus said to the seventy-two after they had returned from their missionary journey: that they were also blessed, because of what they saw and heard of God's miracles – because prophets and kings before them had desired to see and hear what they had heard, but it was not given to them.

Thus, we are blessed when we believe with our hearts even though we have not seen, but we are also blessed when we can taste and see what the prophets and kings were denied.

When we consider that many of us have the opportunity to be present at the Holy Mass more than ten thousand times during our life (and maybe much more, even 20,000 times), we realise how important even the slightest experience is, how important it is to try to get to know Jesus at the Holy Mass, and how important it is to receive Holy Communion with the right disposition of heart. If the grace of the Father at every Mass would just attract us a little more each time, very soon we would be able to enjoy His presence increasingly. I truly feel that we have to push and push for the grace to experience God's presence to take place in our soul at every Mass. It will happen if we recognise that the peak of the Mass is a true encounter with the living Jesus in the Eucharist.

Communion is not just a "reward" that Jesus gives us after we have confessed our sins. Neither does He come into the souls of those who consider themselves sinless and therefore they *deserve* Communion. He comes to those who need Him, to those who love Him. He comes to those who really believe that He comes in the flesh, as a true God and true man. He comes to those who wish to partake of Him as the Sacrificial Lamb.

Those who need Him are far more numerous than those who truly love Him, but He still comes because He knows that love often begins with received grace. He is the One who loves first always. That is why in our relationship with Him we should not dwell too much on how to deserve His love – it is enough to think about how to return His love.

One of the offertory prayers says that an exchange takes place in Communion in which Jesus takes (redeems) our fallen nature in order for us to become part of His divine nature. Which is why, in the same prayer, we ask to be able *to really recognise and live* this truth. We can understand with our minds what the Bible and the Church say of Holy Communion, but we will not live it unless we sense this truth in our hearts, unless we experience it. That's why we must yearn for this understanding, and that is why we pray this last invocation before receiving:

Lord, I am not worthy to have You enter under my roof; but only say the word and I shall be healed.

This invocation, which in its context means something different, we can interpret today as:

Lord, when You come into me, grant me that I experience at least one word in my heart because Your word can change me, it can heal and free me.

Lord, can I be worthy if my heart doesn't yearn for Your word?!

I think that at the end of our lives, we will be bitterly saddened by all the lost opportunities that were offered to us in a special way in Holy Communion.

(CCC 1382; CCC 1391-1396; CCC 1374; CCC 1377; CCC 1098; SC 11; EE 61; CCC 1355; Jn. 20:29; Lk. 10:24; Jn. 3:16; 1 Jn. 4:10-11; Jn. 17:23-26; 1 Cor. 11:28-31)

PREPARING ONESELF TO RECEIVE THE GRACES OF HOLY MASS

The assembly should prepare itself to encounter its Lord and to become "a people well disposed." The preparation of hearts is the joint work of the Holy Spirit and the assembly, especially of its ministers. The grace of the Holy Spirit seeks to awaken faith, conversion of heart, and adherence to the Father's will. These dispositions are the precondition both for the reception of other graces conferred in the celebration itself and the fruits of new life which the celebration is intended to produce afterward.

(CCC 1098)

The Church teaches us that the preparation for the Holy Mass is absolutely necessary if we wish to participate actively and beneficially. I myself am convinced of this after years and years of attending Masses. Jesus Christ participated absolutely and completely in His passion: with His whole heart, His whole soul, with the whole of his physical, mental, and spiritual strength. He redeemed us with His passion, death and resurrection because He loves us, because He cares about us. If we want to participate beneficially, first of all, we have to love and we have to care, firstly about our intimate relationship with Him and then about the person we will offer the Mass for. And we should at least try to participate in the Mass with our whole heart, our whole soul, and with the whole strength of our will (Mt. 22:35-38).

We will certainly not achieve what we want at every Mass, but God does not only look at what we achieve. He is really interested in what we wanted to expect and achieve, what are the real aims of our hearts. He is interested in the amount of love we put into our participation.

For this reason, I try to reach inside myself, to see what the true desires and thoughts of my heart are, what it is that I really want to achieve with the offering of Jesus' sacrifice. In time, many of my intentions became much clearer, and I do not need as much time in order to dispose my heart towards an efficient offering. This is how it is with such fruitful offerings of the Mass. For example, if I hear that someone is nearing death, a few minutes is sufficient to prepare myself and focus on the Holy Mass.

I hope that no one is discouraged by the length of the texts which I am suggesting. They are very soon written into the heart, and before the Mass it is enough to call them to mind. My desire is to realise an audio format of the following texts in order to let everyone benefit from them and become used to these kind of prayers.

Preparation should, by grace of the Spirit, achieve a disposition of openness to faith of the heart, a yearning for conversion (for a quality change of heart) and a readiness for acceptance of what the Father is offering as a fruit of Jesus' sacrifice and fruit of our dwelling in Him. (CCC 1098; CCC 1128).

Christ redeemed us in His love from the cross. By willingly offering our own suffering (sacrifices), we show our love for Jesus and towards our neighbour in need. The offering of our own sacrifices is an act and prayer which unites us with the crucified Christ in a particular way.

Which is why in the days that we offer the Mass, we unite ourselves with the crucified Christ, and we show both ourselves and God that we really care about the person we are offering the Mass for (Col. 1:24-26). It is important that the sacrifice is made out of pure love towards God, and the person we are praying for, and if possible, this should be in secrecy.

Here are some of the sacrifices suitable for offering during Mass in order for us to be one with Christ's sacrifice: fasting, abstaining from something that we like (television, Internet, coffee, cigarettes, hobbies...), doing acts of mercy which we do not usually do, abstaining from grumbling, complaining or gossiping...

In order to get as much as possible out of our preparation, we have to go through the Mass text with understanding and with heart. We have to read and meditate the text over and over again until we have conceived it at least in our understanding and that we heartily desire everything written in it. When that happens, we need a lot less effort and time.

At Mass, there are several different invocations which like Ezekiel's dry bones will need to have meat put on them. When we pronounce them, we must breathe life into these words, we have to infuse them with our offertory intentions (Ez. 37:1-8). When, for example, at the Mass, we say the words *"Lamb of God, who takes away the sins of the world, have mercy upon us"*, we have to be aware of what we are praying. We must really wish the Lamb of God to take pity on us. In the Act of Contrition, we have to be aware of what we are asking for forgiveness. In the Gloria, we have to be aware of what we are really thankful for, why are we glorifying, blessing, adoring, and what we are seeking.

During preparation, sometimes there will be parts that we will only be able to accept in our heads. It will feel incomplete. We will be aware that some of the things we said still have not been completely accepted or convinced in our hearts, like when we have to completely forgive someone who hurt us very deeply from the bottom of our hearts. Or when we declare that we are surrendering ourselves to the will of God and not being sure if we are able to accept the possibility that maybe it is not going to go the way we hoped. We will be able to accept it at the time of the Mass. When I say "able to accept", I do not mean able to accept intense suffering. The type of acceptance I am talking about is best expressed in the idea: "joyful realisation with which our whole being agrees with happiness."

It is important to realise that *the engraving, the preparation in our hearts*, is a process that takes time. The length of time very much depends on how much we want this. The more we want it, the less time it will take us to reach it, because preparation is enabled by the strength of our will. Of course, none of us is perfect. If all that preparation seems too difficult and too long for us, if we feel that, in the moment, we do not have enough willpower to do it seriously, we can try again when some other situation in life, which affects us more deeply, comes along (either our own or someone else's that we really care about).

In a good preparation, the standard "formula" prayers are also useful. These are devotions that are used in the majority of parishes before the Holy Mass such as the rosary or different litanies. What is important is that those prayers are not just recited or listed off, but rather that they are prayed with understanding and with the heart. We will not be heard just because of many words (Mt. 6:6-8). Those individual invocations which we pondered during our preparation for the Mass must be repeated with understanding within our spirits and must resound in our hearts. So, for example, if we prayed "Holy Mary, Mother of God, pray for us sinners", we become aware that we are asking her to pray for what we were thinking about during our preparation. We do the same thing for different parts of the litany. In this way, we become aware of the real presence, the role, the help and support of the saints with the Blessed Virgin at the lead. At the same time, these prayers help us to create habits in our heart that, at certain rites and invocations, we can unite our intentions with greater ease. It also helps us to participate in the Mass with undivided attention.

Besides the rosary and the litanies, inspired singing with suitable songs is an excellent preparation for the Mass. It is also good to have Eucharistic adoration as a preparation. Because this disposes our heart even more towards the culmination of the Mass which is the Eucharist. If the priest puts a small host into the monstrance before the Mass, with which the believers make Communion, this can be a great help to them especially when he takes this host afterwards and puts it in front of them into the ciborium, from which the believers will be served. In this way, their attention is drawn even more to the holiness of the act of making Communion with our Lord. Man is a psychological creature and that is why we have the sacraments, which are visible signs of invisible greater realities, i.e. God's mysterious presence among us.

Of course, there are other means of preparing for the Eucharist, such as confession, meditation on God's Word, meditation on the Passion etc.

Personally, I like to set aside an hour before morning Mass to listen or to read the Gospel. I like to see with my own eyes and hear with my own ears the Person I will meet and receive at the Holy Mass. My encounter with Him at Mass will greatly depend on the degree to which I experienced Him in my preparation.

At the same time, whenever I can, I like to spend at least half an hour after Mass when I get home, meditating on the Word of God. I like to give Him this time because this is a special precious time when I am so much at peace within myself and so it is easier to hear, recognise and accept the Word that He has for me – words which build me up and make me a better person.

It is important to note that I, personally, at every Holy Mass expect the grace that will change me, which will spiritually lift me up, to put it "vividly", at least by "only" an inch. Sometimes that one inch, that one little grace I receive, is enough to keep my head above water and keep me from drowning. After many Holy Masses, inches slowly become yards (or metres). I tend to think more and more about eternity and I truly tend to enjoy God's presence more and more. I become more and more aware of my weaknesses and I tend to rely more and more on God's grace. And, as one congregational Mass prayer says, I become more and more deeply aware that God's grace is so often our only hope and that God's protection is our only security (Fifth Sunday in ordinary time, congregational). If we despise that one inch, if we think that one inch is not worth the good effort to prepare for the Holy Mass, then we may still be at zero, we may still be coming to Holy Mass simply out of obligation. Probably we will come out from the Mass the same as when we went to it – we come from it without experiencing grace.

The following pages offer some specific steps for preparation which I think will be useful to the reader. I put these preparations aside for myself and some of my friends who asked for help with their special intentions. Readers can use these preparations in full. They can add or remove at will what does not apply to them or they can use them as an inspiration as to how to make their own preparations.

Personally, I always like adding or removing something, depending on the momentary inspirations that I receive in prayer. That is why these suggested preparations have no set framework or structure, nor should they have. What is important is that, in every preparation, at least some little piece of the text should enter us and remain with us. It is important to be completely relaxed when we begin, without specific expectations in our hearts, because we never know in what way the Spirit will inspire us and put something in our hearts. God knows us truly, completely and perfectly, and He knows whatever we need at a given moment. Which is why, whenever we feel certain words echoing in our hearts in a particular way, we should stop and quietly repeat them, over and over, until we feel it is time to continue with the rest of the preparation.

If we really care about the person we are offering the Mass for, there is no need to be afraid. The Holy Spirit will help us very much and we will be able to recognise His guidance, His leading, not just at the time of preparation, but also during the Mass.

PRAYING FOR LIBERATION FROM PURGATORY

Lord, Your Son died for us on the cross and rose again. In this Eucharist, we pray for our deceased brothers and sisters. Purify them with this eternal sacrifice that they may enter into the glory of the resurrection. Through Christ Our Lord.
(Prayer after Communion)

(Begin by making the sign of the cross)

May this preparation be in the name of the Father, and of the Son, and of the Holy Spirit! Amen!

May Your grace be with me, Lord Jesus Christ, Your love, God the Father, and Your company, O Holy Spirit.

INTENTION

Eternal Father, I offer You the sacrifice of Your most Beloved Son, our Lord Jesus Christ, for the redemption of X from purgatory (place the name of the person you are offering the Mass for at X).

THANKSGIVING

I thank You, Lord, for the gift of life that You gave X. You miraculously imagined and created X

You created X in Your image and likeness. You created X to live in eternity, giving X this short life to determine his eternity.

In the depths of his soul, You impressed love ready for sacrifice, ready for forgiveness, blessing, and thanksgiving, ready for giving and helping.

You gave X a hint of love, the fullness of which can only be experienced in You.

You, heavenly Father, in the sacrament of baptism, You took X with Your limitless love as Your child and called X to discover this love throughout his life with the help of the Holy Spirit.

Thank You, Lord, for choosing the time and place where X would be born.

Thank You for choosing his/her family and the situation in life in which X was born.

Thank You for every member of his family.

(Name some of them if you know them.)

Thank You for the family that he/she had.

(If X was married, names of the spouse and children.)

And thank You for any other person who was important to X.

Thank You also for all the people who were good to X and to his/her family in any way.

Thank You for those who were a fountain of faith, Lord, of faith in You. For those who taught X about You and spoke of You.

Thank You for all those who blessed X with their prayers.

You gave X many opportunities to choose love in his life, opportunities to show love and respect for You and for his fellow men.

You gave X many opportunities to sacrifice himself/herself in love for others and to forgive many times.

Lord, You gave him many happy times and many good gifts and many opportunities to thank You and glorify You.

Lord, You gave X many opportunities in which he/she needed Your help, because You wanted to draw X to Yourself.

You gave X many opportunities to seek You out and find You, to spend time in Your presence so that he/she would be filled with grace and wisdom.

You wanted his/her joy to grow. You wanted X to store up treasures for Heaven. You wanted X to be as close as possible to You in Heaven.

Thank You, Lord, for every grace that You granted X and which he worked with in his life. Thank You for all his/her good acts, thank You for each and every sacrifices X made from love, thank You for every good word that X uttered, for every good wish that X carried in his/her heart.

Thank You, Lord, for every moment X spent with You and in You. Thank You for every Mass that X attended, for every confession, for every prayer that X uttered from his/her heart.

Lord, You offer us the fullness of life, You offer us Yourself, but we too often choose our own version of the fullness of life with its idols, and we put them before You and before our neighbour.

So, instead of the fullness of life, we choose emptiness; instead of Your Word, we choose empty words and promises.

Lord, despite everything You give us, we remain ungrateful and fall into sin.

Often, we try to justify our sin. Often, our repentance is insincere.

Lord, many of us do not understand in our hearts Your righteousness nor Your mercy and that is why we cannot or we do not want to forgive those who hurt us.

Lord, many of us do not manage to change the way You want us to, because we do not realise that You are the one who gives us a new heart – when we are with You and in You.

Without You, without Your forgiveness, none of us can be saved.

That is why we thank You, Father, for giving us Your only Beloved Son, Jesus Christ, so that anyone who believes in Him can be saved and can have eternal life.

Thank You, Jesus, for paying for our sins and our vices.

Thank You, Lord, for putting X into my heart so that, with love and sincere desire, I can offer Your sacrifice to the Father for his/her liberation from purgatory.

PRAYER

Heavenly Father, I know with how much yearning X would like to offer now the sacrifice of Your Son for his/her own liberation from purgatory, but You in Your justice have ordained that only during our earthly life can we offer Jesus' sacrifice.

This is why I am offering the sacrifice of Your Beloved Son on behalf of X.

Please, Father, forgive his/her sins in my name, his/her name, and in Jesus' name, because I know that X is now fully aware of his/her thoughts and the motives of his/her heart during his life and that X now fully repents and is crying out for Your mercy.

Please, Father, in my name, his/her name, and Jesus' name, with Your mercy and grace, bring peace to those whom X wounded with his sins in any way.

Grant that any evil he/she caused others can be turned to good.

Please, Father, in my and in Jesus' name, forgive those who X during his/her earthly life did not know how, could not or did not want to forgive.

I beg You to fill X with Your holy peace and lead him/her into Your kingdom of love, justice, and peace.

This, Father, is all I pray in Jesus' name, because I know that Jesus died for X out of pure love.

PROFESSION OF FAITH

Lord, You established the sacrament of the Eucharist, so that we could effectively and repeatedly participate in Your sacrifice and reap the fruits of redemption, fruits of love and of mercy.

I thank You for coming to us in the Eucharist as true man and true God, so that we can come to You like people from the Gospels, the one who suffers, the one who is ill, the one who has sinned, to receive Your love and Your mercy.

Jesus, You redeemed us from the consequences of sin. You redeemed our fallen nature enslaved in selfishness and subject to sin.

Your sacrifice is without blemish, and You expect of us that we offer it to the Father both for ourselves and for others.

Lord, I believe that in Your Eucharist I am partaking Your Body and Blood. I will receive You, the Sacrificial Lamb that was killed for our sins.

I believe, Jesus, that You come into me with Your divine and human love.

I believe that You are coming so close to me now so that, with Your grace, You are filling my heart with trust in Your infinite mercy and love towards You and towards X for whom I want to offer this Holy Mass.

Holy Spirit, guide me through this Holy Mass.

Grant that, by Your grace, my thoughts are in harmony with my words.

Grant that X is in my heart throughout this whole Mass.

Thank You, Holy Spirit, for Your help, because without Your grace we cannot pray as we should, nor can we believe in our hearts, and we cannot love with pure love.

Holy Mary, Mother of God, Queen of Peace, pray for me as I offer this sacrifice, and pray for the soul of X for whom I am offering this sacrifice of Your Son.

Mary, you are the one who is most closely connected with Jesus' passion and death. You were His comfort and strength in the toughest moments. And you felt the depth of pain which remained hidden from most people.

Which is why, Mary, I cannot offer the sacrifice of your Son without presenting your sacrifice too, and the sacrifices of all those who throughout the centuries united their suffering with that of your Son. I cannot offer it without presenting my own suffering, however incomparably small it is in comparison with yours.

Mary, pray for me to receive the grace that I recognise more deeply the point of presenting my own renunciations and sacrifices, so that with as much faith and love as possible, I can present this sacrifice of Jesus for the souls of those in need of the grace of redemption.

I thank You, God. I glorify and bless You.

I adore You and thank You for Your infinite goodness.

Because You alone are the Holy One.

You alone are the Lord.

You alone are the Most High, Jesus Christ.

With the Holy Spirit, in the glory of God the Father.

Amen.

COMMUNION MEDITATION

Lord Jesus, Lamb of God, I am not worthy for You to come under my roof, I am not worthy for You to enter my soul, but I still pray that You fill me with Your presence.

Because, Lord, how can I become worthy by myself?

How can I light a lamp in my soul, Lord, if you are the Light, when You are the only one who can light up my darkness? Only You can make me see with my heart, hear with my heart, understand with my heart, so that I can sincerely repent and accept You who are the Light.

How can I forgive, Lord, without Your grace? How can I sincerely repent, how can I pray with faith, how can I change?

How can I, Lord, without You, who are the one true Peace, bring peace to my soul?

Lord, how can my soul live if You, who are Life, do not live in it?

Lord, how can my unworthy soul love if You, who are the Teacher, do not dwell within it, if Love does not dwell there?

Lord, how can I be grateful, how can I glorify You, how can I bless You, if my unworthy soul does not taste Your holy presence, if it does not feel Your peace or Your joy?

Come, Lord, as my Redeemer and my Saviour, as my doctor and healer, come in and be King of my heart.

Come, Jesus, say the Word, and my whole being will be made whole.

Come, Jesus, in me, pull me to Your cross, pull me into Your heart, because I want to give You my pains and my sickness, because I want to give You my wounded heart.

Come, Jesus, and teach me to love, the way You loved us.

Come, Jesus, because I want to pray with You, with Your love to the Father, so He will have mercy on those I am offering this Mass for.

Amen.

PRAYING FOR **THE SALVATION OF THE DYING**

Almighty and merciful God! You show love to the whole of creation. Hear the prayer of our dying brethren: Redeemed by the precious blood of Your Son, may they pass from this world without the stain of sin and rest in Your fatherly embrace. Through our Lord.
(Collect prayer)

(Begin by making the sign of the cross.)

May this preparation be in the name of the Father, and of the Son, and of the Holy Spirit! Amen!

May Your grace be with me, Lord Jesus Christ, Your love, God the Father, and Your company, O Holy Spirit.

INTENTION

Eternal Father, I offer You the sacrifice of Your most Beloved Son, our Lord Jesus Christ, for the redemption of X who is near death (place the name of the person you are offering the Mass for at X).

THANKSGIVING

I thank You, Lord, for the gift of life that You gave X. You miraculously imagined and created X.

You created X in Your image and likeness.

You created X to live in eternity, giving X this short life to determine his/her eternity.

In the depths of his/her soul, You impressed love, readiness for sacrifice, readiness for forgiveness, blessing and thanksgiving, for giving and helping.

You gave X a hint of love, the fullness of which can only be experienced in You.

You, heavenly Father, in the sacrament of baptism, took X with boundless love as Your child and called X to discover this love throughout his/her life with the help of the Holy Spirit.

Thank You, Lord, for choosing the time and place where X would be born.

Thank You for choosing his/her family and the situation in life in which X was born.

Thank You for every member of his/her family.

(Name some of them if you know them.)

Thank You for the family that he/she had.

(If X was married, names of the spouse and children.)

And thank You for any other person who was important to X.

Thank You also for all the people who were good to x and to his/her family in any way.

Thank You for those who were a fountain of faith, Lord, of faith in You. For those who taught X about You and spoke of You.

Thank You for all those who blessed X with their prayers and still pray for X.

You gave X many opportunities to choose love in his/her life, opportunities to show love and respect for You and for his/her fellow men.

You gave X many opportunities to sacrifice himself/herself out of love for others and to forgive many times.

Lord, You gave X many happy times and many good gifts, and many opportunities to thank You and glorify You.

Lord, You allowed X many opportunities in which X needed Your help, because You wanted to draw X to Yourself.

You gave X many opportunities to seek You out and find You, to spend time in Your presence so that X would be filled with grace and wisdom.

I want to thank You, God, for every grace that X received, thank You for every good deed that X did. Thank You for every sacrifice that X made out of love, thank You for every good word that X uttered. Thank You for every good desire that X carried in his heart.

Thank You, Lord, for every moment X spent with You and in You. Thank You for every Mass that X attended, for every confession, for every prayer that X uttered from his/her heart.

You Lord wanted his/her joy to increase, You wanted X to accumulate incorruptible treasure for eternal life, You wanted X to be as close as possible to You in eternity.

Lord, You offer us the fullness of life, You offer us Yourself, but we too often choose our own version of the fullness of life with its idols and we put them before You and before our neighbour.

So instead of the fullness of life, we choose emptiness; instead of Your Word, empty words and promises.

Lord, despite everything You give us, we remain ungrateful and fall into sin.

Often, we try to justify our sin. Often, our repentance is insincere.

Lord, many of us do not understand Your righteousness in our hearts nor Your mercy, and that's why we cannot or we do not want to forgive those who hurt us.

Lord, many of us do not manage to change the way You want us to, because we know that You are the one who gives us a new heart – when we are with You and in You.

Without You, without Your forgiveness, none of us can be saved.

That is why we thank You, Father, for giving us Your only Beloved Son, Jesus Christ, so that anyone who believes in Him can be saved and can have eternal life.

Thank You for promising us that whoever calls on Your name will be saved.

Thank You, Lord, for putting X into my heart so that, with love and sincere desire, I can offer Your sacrifice to the Father in order to draw X to Your love on the cross, so that Your grace will illuminate his/her heart and mind.

PRAYER

Heavenly Father, please draw X to Yourself with the love of Your Son who sacrificed Himself on the cross for his salvation.

Grant X the grace that he/she can and wishes to receive You as King of his heart, that X wants You as his/her personal Saviour and Redeemer – so that Jesus can raise him/her up on the last day.

Nobody can come to Jesus, Saviour and Redeemer, if You, Father, who sent Him into the world, do not draw them to Him (Jn. 6:44).

I ask You, Father, in Jesus' name, grant him the light of Your Spirit so that he/she clearly see the secret thoughts and motives of his/her heart by which X lived; so that X wishes to sincerely repent for his/her sins; so that X can seek and receive forgiveness.

Grant X, Lord, the grace that he/she can and wishes to see those whom X hurt by his sins, and so he can sincerely pray for them.

Please, Father, in Jesus' name, grant X the grace that he/she can and wishes to forgive those who hurt X in his/her life, all of those who denied him/her love and respect.

I ask You to grant X the grace to forgive himself/herself.

My Lord, surround X by Your grace so that X can be free from the attacks of the evil one, so X can be free from pride and hurt, and anything else that would make him/her refuse Your mercy.

I beg You, Lord, to find a way to come to his/her heart.

I beg You in the name of Jesus to fill his/her soul with Your holy peace and joy and grant him the grace of the Holy Spirit so that X can thank You, glorify You, and bless You.

Grant X the grace that he/she would want to die with the consolation of the holy sacraments.

Please, Lord, fill X with Your holy peace and lead X into the kingdom of love, peace, and justice.

Lord Jesus, You established the sacrament of the Eucharist so that we could effectively and repeatedly participate in Your sacrifice and reap the fruits of redemption, fruits of love and of mercy.

I thank You that You come to us in the Eucharist as a true man and true God, so that we can come to You like people from the gospels, like the one who suffers, the one who is ill, the one who has sinned, to receive Your love and Your mercy.

Jesus, You redeemed us from the consequences of sin. You redeemed our fallen nature enslaved in selfishness and subject to sin.

Your sacrifice is without blemish, and You expect of us that we offer it to the Father both for ourselves and for others.

Lord, I believe that in Your Eucharist I am partaking of Your Body and Blood. I will receive You, the Sacrificial Lamb that was killed for our sins.

Jesus, I believe that You come to me with Your divine and human love.

And I want to come unto You as well with all my human misery.

I believe that you come so close to me now so that, with Your grace, You fill my heart with trust in Your infinite mercy and love towards You and towards X for whom I want to offer this Holy Mass.

Holy Spirit, guide me through this Holy Mass.

Grant that, by Your grace, my thoughts are in harmony with my words.

Grant that X is in my heart throughout this whole Mass.

Thank You, Holy Spirit, for Your help, because without Your grace we cannot pray as we should, we cannot believe in our hearts, and we cannot love with pure love.

My Angel, protect my thoughts and feelings during this Holy Mass so that I am continuously with God and in God.

Holy Mary, Mother of God, Queen of Peace, pray for me as I offer this Mass and pray for the soul of the person that I am offering the sacrifice of your Son.

Mary, you are the one who is most closely connected with Jesus' passion and death. You stood underneath His cross. You were His comfort and strength in the toughest moments. And you felt the depth of pain which remained hidden from most people.

Which is why, Mary, I cannot offer the sacrifice of your Son without presenting your sacrifice too, and the sacrifices of all those who, throughout the centuries, united their suffering with that of your Son, and without presenting my own suffering, however incomparably small it is in comparison with yours.

Holy Mary, Mother of God, bring to your dying Son the person for whose salvation I am offering His sacrifice to the Father. May your love, Mary, pierce the part of his or her soul which is incapable of rejecting your love. May your love, Mary, attract him or her so that they can believe in your mercy and can call on to His name.

Mary, pray for me to receive the grace to recognise even more deeply the point of presenting my own renunciations and sacrifices so that, with as much faith and love as possible, I can present this sacrifice of Jesus for the souls of those who are in need of the grace of redemption.

Saint Joseph, you experienced a blessed death because you lived with uprightness, because you believed in Jesus as Saviour, and because both Jesus and Mary were present at your death.

Saint Joseph, Protector of the Dying, pray for X so that he/she can die in peace, helped by the sacraments, and justified by the Blood of the Lamb.

Souls in purgatory, pray for me so that I pray this Mass with as much fervour as possible. And I will pray for you, souls, at the offertory, conscious that one day I may call out for prayers from purgatory as well.

I thank You, God. I glorify and bless You.

I adore You and thank You for Your infinite goodness.

Because You alone are the Holy One.

You alone are the Lord.

You alone are the Most High, Jesus Christ.

With the Holy Spirit, in the glory of God the Father.

COMMUNION MEDITATION

Lord Jesus, Lamb of God, I am not worthy for You to come under my roof, I am not worthy for You to enter my soul, but I am still praying that You will fill me with Your presence.

Because, Lord, how can I become worthy by myself?

How can I light a lamp in my soul, Lord, if you are the Light, when You are the only one who can light up my darkness, only You can make me see with the heart, hear with my heart, understand with my heart, so that I can sincerely repent and accept You who are the Light?

How can I, Lord, forgive without Your grace? How will I sincerely repent, how can I pray with faith, how will I change?

How can I, Lord, without You, who are the one true Peace, bring peace to my soul?

Lord, how can my soul live if You, who are Life, do not live in it?

Lord, how can my unworthy soul love if You, who are the Teacher, do not dwell within it, if Love does not dwell there?

Lord, how can I be grateful, how can I glorify You, how can I bless You, if my unworthy soul does not taste Your holy presence, if it does not feel Your peace or Your joy?

Come, Lord, as my Redeemer and my Saviour, as my Doctor and Healer, come in and be King of my heart.

Come, Jesus, in me, pull me to Your cross, pull me into Your heart, because I want to give You my pains and my wounded heart.

Come, Jesus, say the Word and my whole being will be made whole.

Come, Jesus, and teach me to love, the way You loved us.

Come, Jesus, because I want to pray with You, with Your love to the Father, so He will have mercy on those I am offering this mass for.

Amen.

CONCLUSION

I BELIEVE THAT THE MASS can be offered in this way for those who have already died, regardless how long it has been since their death. In advance, God would have seen our heartfelt prayer, and I do not think there is any reason for Him not to accept it. This is especially important for those who died without the sacraments, or for those who died under trauma, and for all those who we are not sure if they were in the grace of God.

I believe that the offerings for such intentions are a great act of mercy for anyone whom we decide to offer it for. Definitely, every one of us, at the moment of death, would like to have someone who will intercede for us before Jesus with faith and love. This is the reason why we say in the *Hail, Mary* "pray for us, sinners, now and at the hour of our death."

Many times, I have been inspired before Mass to offer the Mass in this way. Sometimes, it is for someone who has been dead for a long time. It must be then that this is an effective way of helping those who in some cases would have no one to intercede for them, and so aid them in their salvation. We should always remember those who died without the sacrament of confession, but also those who died alone, without family and friends, those who died in great pain, in hatred, with feelings of rejection, guilt and disappointment, those, for example, who took their own lives.

Sometimes, when I am praying this way, the Holy Spirit puts other people in my heart so that I can unite my prayers for them for the same intention. I firmly believe that sometimes one prayer said from the heart is enough to save someone. And when we are in God, we are praying with our whole heart.

PRAYING FOR OUR OWN REDEMPTION FROM ILLNESS

Almighty and Eternal God, salvation of all believers! We call upon Your mercy for our sick: bring them back to health and grant that they render thanks to You in Your Church. Through the Lord.
(Collect prayer: for the sick)

(We begin with the sign of the cross.)

May this preparation be in the name of the Father, and of the Son, and of the Holy Spirit!

May Your grace be with me, Lord Jesus Christ, Your love, God my Father, and Your anointing, Holy Spirit.

INTENTION

Eternal Father, I offer the sacrifice of Your Beloved Son, our Lord Jesus Christ, for the redemption of my sickness (mention illness here).

THANKSGIVING

I thank You, Lord, for the gift of life.

You created me awesomely in Your likeness and image. You created me for eternity giving me the opportunity in this short life to determine how my life would be in eternity.

In the depths of my soul, You impressed love, made me ready for sacrifice, ready to forgive, to bless and thank; ready for giving and helping.

You impressed love in me which can only be felt in You.

You received me, heavenly Father, in baptism with limitless love as Your adopted son/daughter and You invited me to discover and live that love during my life with the help of the Holy Spirit.

(Call on the Holy Spirit now and remain in this prayer for as long as you feel it is necessary.)

Thank You, Lord, for choosing the place and time of my birth.

(Mention your date of birth.)

Thank You for choosing the family and the situation in life in which I was born.

Thank You for every member of my family.

(Remember every member of your family individually.)

Thank You for every person in my life who was important to me.

(Remember some of them.)

Thank You for any of those who did good to me.

(Remember some of them.)

Thank You, O Lord, for those who were an example of faith to me, who taught me about You or spoke to me about You.

(Remember some of them.)

Thank You for inspiring me to seek You and find You: in prayer, in the Sacred Scripture, in the sacraments, in religious books, in those around me who need Your mercy...

Thank You, Lord, that I often dwell in You so that I can be filled anew with Your love, faith, peace, joy, wisdom, goodness, strength...

Thank You, my Saviour, that You are ready to enter every situation in life that I invite You into with my whole heart.

(Call Him now in your own words into your situation in life.)

You sent me Your Holy Spirit, Lord, so that I could repeatedly be filled with His grace to dwell in You over and over again and remain within You.

When I am in You, Lord, You give me rest. You liberate me, You heal my spirit, soul, and body. You teach me and change me. When I am in You, You give me Your love with which I can forgive everyone and sacrifice myself for others. When I am in You, my Redeemer, You give me faith in my heart and pure love with which I can pray for everyone. When I am in You, You give me strength of the will with which I can stop sinning and continue on the path of salvation.

When I am in You, Eternal Father, You fill me with peace and joy and the fullness of life.

Lord, You offer me the fullness of life. You offer me Yourself, but I often choose a different version of the fullness of life, and I place my own idols above You and above my neighbour.

I know, Lord, that without You, without Your forgiveness, I cannot be saved.

That is why I thank You, Father, for giving us Your only Beloved Son, Jesus Christ, so that anyone who believes in Him can be saved, and can have eternal life.

Thank You, Jesus, because You, instead of me, paid the punishment for my sins and my wantonness.

Thank You because, while suffering and dying on the cross, You took my pains upon You, my humiliation, my wounds, and my fears.

Thank You for taking my sickness and healing me with Your wounds.

Thank You, Lord, for your immeasurable love towards the downtrodden, the despised, the rejected, the sick, and the suffering.

Thank You, God, for Your fatherly love for us, repentant sinners.

Lord Jesus, You instituted the Eucharist so that I too could participate over and over again in Your redeeming passion, so that I could reap the fruits of redemption, so that I can grow in love, grace, and wisdom.

(Think of someone else that you want to include in your intention, especially the sick people you know.)

Thank You for coming to me in the Eucharist in which I can abandon my illness to You so that You can carry it on Your cross and heal me with Your wounds.

(Hand over your illness and He will do what is best for you.)

Thank You, because in the Eucharist You come to me as true God and true man, so that I, like the people from the Gospel, the sick, the suffering and the sinners, can come to You, become united with You, so that we can gain Your grace of redemption.

Thank You, Lord, for all those who care for us, sick people. Thank You for the doctors, the nurses, and all those who do research on new medication. Thank You for those who pray for us, who bear witness to their faith and who offer sacrifices. (Think of all those who dedicate their lives to caring for the sick and thank God for all of them.)

Thank You, loving Father, for sending me an angel to serve me and counsel me on the road to salvation.

(Thank your angel from the bottom of your heart.)

Thank You for the help of the saints who gladly hear our prayers that we address to them with faith.

(Thank the saints you pray to.)

Most of all, I thank You for the help and intercession of our and my mother, the Blessed Virgin Mary.

(Here, pray at least one Hail Mary with your heart for everything she has done for you up till now.)

REPENTANCE

First of all, Lord, I bring You my sorrow for my sins.

Only You, Lord, know all my sins. Only You know about my lack of forgiveness towards those who hurt me and contributed to my illness.

Forgive me my unwillingness to forgive.

Lord, only You know how much I damaged my health by my disordered and irresponsible life.

(Remember here your intolerance and other sins with which you damaged your health.)

Forgive me.

Only You know how ungrateful I was for all those days when I enjoyed the fullness of health.

Forgive me.

Only You, Father, know how I used my health when I had it.

(Think back on how your relationship with God and neighbour was then and how it should be changed if Jesus were to give you back your health.)

Forgive me.

Lord, only You know how many times I sinned with my thoughts, words, and deeds.

Forgive me.

Only You know how many sins of omission I have committed, when I passed over a chance to do good and avoid a chance to act badly (Remember those sins).

Forgive me, Lord Jesus.

Only You know how many times I have hurt others, consciously or unconsciously, how much pain I have brought, especially to those who are dear to me.

(Remember those situations and repent.)

Forgive me.

I ask You, Lord, by Your grace, to enable all those whom I hurt to forgive me.

I beg You to redeem them from the consequences of my sin and heal their wounds, and with Your peace repair the pain that I caused them.

(Remember some of them.)

FORGIVENESS

Lord, only You know how many times I refused to forgive those who hurt me.

(Remember those whom you still have not forgiven).

Forgive me, Lord.

Only You know how many times, because of hurt and pride, although I did not want it to be that way, I could not forgive.

Forgive me for not coming to You then, when Your grace would have helped me to forgive.

Lord, You told us that without You we can do nothing.

Lord, I am before You now, I am with You, and I really want to forgive all of those who sinned against me.

Please, Lord, forgive all of those who hurt me, with lies, with gossip, swearing, judging, humiliating, manipulating, maltreating, with their coarseness, deceptions, and unfulfilled promises.

(Remember some of them and forgive them.)

Please, forgive me too when I committed these sins against others.

(Remember some of them.)

Forgive me, Lord, for all the broken promises that I made to You, to others and to myself.

(Remember some of them)

I wish to forgive and, together with You, forgive anyone that I know who hurt me, but also those that I do not know who sinned against me.

Lord, I want to forgive and, with Your grace, really forgive those who are sorry and who repent, but even those who are not sorry and do not repent for hurting me.

Lord, I forgive those who were not conscious that they brought me pain.

My God, I forgive all.

(In your heart, now repeat over and over: "I forgive, I forgive, I forgive.")

Lord, I forgive because I too often sin, and I too wish to be forgiven.

Lord, I forgive because I want my heart to be cleansed, because I want to live in Your peace, because I want to live in Your dignity.

Lord, I forgive everyone because You created all of us with the same love and You await that everyone of us, sinners, convert and live.

Jesus, I believe that I will taste the fullness of Your forgiving grace in an encounter with You in the Eucharist – if we experience the love with which You loved us as You hung on the cross.

Thank You, Jesus, because You promised that I would not be judged if I do not judge others, and that my sins are forgiven if I forgive others.

PRAYER

You came to give rest to the tired and the burdened. You came to heal the brokenhearted, to heal all illness, all inabilities in Your people. You came to redeem and free all those whom the devil is torturing.

Having died on the cross, You took my pain upon Yourself, You carried my illness, You paid for my sins and my wretchedness, and with Your wounds You healed me.

Jesus, You are the same yesterday, today, and forever.

Jesus, You still walk on this earth today, doing good to those who come to You, and that is why my eyes are focused on You.

Lord Jesus, You know what spiritual illnesses are binding me. You know what are the things that provoke my lack of peace. You know what it is that takes my joy away.

Redeem me, Lord, heal me. Give me the medication I need and set me free.

You know, Lord, what are the wounds which cause me to be ill. You know what are the wounds that block me from loving my neighbour in the way I would like to. You know the reason why I cannot let them completely love me.

(Allow the spirit to bring to my mind what it is that must be healed.)

Redeem me, Lord, heal me, give me the medication I need and set me free.

Please, Lord, redeem me from fear and anxiety.

I beg You, Lord, my Saviour, redeem me from fear and anxiety.

Lord, my Saviour, redeem me from depression, self-pity and self-accusation.

Please, Lord, forgive me for every contact, small or big I had with the satanic kingdom.

(Remember those sins and repent with all your heart.)

Please, Lord, forgive others too if they harmed me by using occult powers and practices.

(In your heart, repeat over and over: "I forgive, I forgive, I forgive...")

Lord, my God, conscious that I am in Your presence, under Your complete protection, with my whole being, I renounce any satanic powers, attachments and bondages and I ask You now with Your Precious Blood that You completely liberate me:

- from every influence of fortune telling
- from every influence of casting spells
- from every influence of sorcery
- from every influence of divination
- from every influence of witchcraft
- from every influence of cursing

Jesus, please drive away far from me any spirit that causes illness, and forbid it from ever returning.

(If there are any strong reactions, give thanks to God and glorify Him, keep repeating the text until there is complete peace in the soul.)

May Your Blood, Lord, wash my conscience and my spirit and soul from these deeds because I wish to be clean before You, because I want only You to be King of my life and my heart.

(For a while, repeat in your heart: "Be my King, be my King, be my King.")

SURRENDER

Lord Jesus Christ, I surrender my illness to You, I surrender my life and I ask You to come into my heart as my Redeemer and Saviour, to come into my life as the Doctor of my soul and of my whole being.

May Your will be done.

You Jesus be King of my life and my heart.

Lord, You can give me health and opportunity for a new life.

Lord, You can give me an understanding of the value of suffering united to Your suffering and so give me a new motive for living.

Lord, You can give me true repentance, you can cleanse me from sin and bring me into Your eternal kingdom of love, justice, and peace.

Lord, if You heal me, grant me the grace to use my health for eternal good.

And if You give me the grace to recognise the value of suffering, grant me humility so that I will not become proud.

If You, Lord, bring me to Yourself, grant my loved ones the knowledge that I will always be with them with intercession and that death is not a loss, just a short separation until we meet again in Heaven. Grant my loved ones firm faith in You and in eternal life – so that our joy in eternity would be complete.

Beloved Father, I beg of You, while I am offering the sacrifice of Your Beloved Son, grant me peace, grant me the grace of patience and the grace of perseverance while I offer my suffering, which I want to unite with Jesus' redeeming sacrifice and offer it for those whom I have hurt with my sins as well as for other sick people and sufferers who are in need of Your mercy.

(Here, remember those you have wounded, and others who are ill and you care about them and you want to offer the Mass sacrifice for them.)

In this, give me Your wisdom and humility.

(Remain at least a minute in complete silence of thought. There is no need to think much. Just be aware that you are in the beloved presence of God.)

PROFESSION OF FAITH

Lord, I believe that at this Mass I will listen to Your Word, I believe You will speak to me, that You will comfort and encourage me.

Lord, I believe that You will draw me to Yourself throughout the whole Mass.

I believe that You want all of my attention and my whole heart focused on You, I believe that You want me to immerse the whole of myself in You.

My Jesus, I believe that You want me to taste Your peace, Your goodness, Your nearness, Your care. I believe that at this Holy Mass You want me to enjoy Your holy presence.

Lord Jesus, my Saviour and Redeemer, I firmly believe that in Communion I will receive Your Body and Blood. I will receive You, the Sacrificial Lamb that was killed for us.

I believe that in Communion You come to me as true God and true man, with Your divine and human love.

I believe that You come to me with Your will, and I with my will want to dwell in You.

I believe that Communion, in which You are in me and I am in You, is the fountain and centre of my life.

Lord, I would like to focus all my attention on You during Communion, and to love You with my whole heart. I want to totally surrender myself to Your goodness and love.

I would like to embrace You, Lord, on Your cross and surrender my sickness to You.

I would like to give You all my needs, Lord, and to surrender the needs of all my loved ones and those who have asked for my prayers.

(Remember those for whom you want to intercede for the grace of redemption, especially some sick persons that you know.)

Above all, my God, I wish to thank You. I want to glorify You, and I want to enjoy Your presence.

I wish that, while I am loving You in these moments, that I learn to love my neighbour too.

I bless You, Lord. I bless Your grace that I will taste and experience at all the Masses in which I will present this intention to the Father, until He grants it.

Thank You that, during every Holy Mass, You will be preparing me up until my total surrender to You.

Holy Spirit, please guide me through this Holy Mass.

Grant by Your grace that my thoughts are in harmony with my words.

Please give me the grace to totally surrender myself to the will of the Father and so receive redemption.

Thank You, Holy Spirit, for You helping me, because without Your grace I do not know how to pray at all.

My guardian angel, keep close watch over my thoughts and feelings during this Holy Mass, so that they are in God and with God.

O Blessed Virgin, Mother of God, Queen of Peace, pray for me. Mary, you are the one who is most connected to Jesus' passion and death. You stood under the cross and you were a comfort and strength in His most terrible moments. You were able to feel the depths of His pain which was hidden from others.

Mary, you are like the prophet Isaiah who could see Jesus taking all our pain and sickness upon Himself, you could see how His wounds heal us.

Mary, you also saw all of those for whom His sacrifice was pointless, those who would have to suffer because they did not trust and they did not hand over their sins their pains, and their illnesses to your Son.

Holy Mary, Mother of God and my Mother, pray for me for the grace to be able to completely trust in His mercy, and receive the fullness of redemption so that His, your and my joy can be complete.

Mary, I cannot offer the sacrifice of your Son without presenting your sacrifice too and without offering the suffering of all those who, throughout the ages, united their suffering with your Son's suffering on the cross. Teach me to offer my own renunciations and suffering regardless of how trivial they look in front of your eyes.

May your love, Mary, reach my soul and may your motherly love release me so that I can totally trust in the mercy of your Son Jesus.

Pray, Mary, for the grace that I understand deeply the importance of offering my own renunciations and sacrifices so that with increasing faith and love I can offer Jesus' sacrifice for the souls who need the grace of redemption the most.

Saint Joseph, holy favourite of God, pray for me.

All of you, my favourite saints... help me by interceding for me before the throne of God.

O Holy Souls, pray for me so that I may participate in the Holy Mass with utmost fervour.

I praise You, Jesus. I glorify You and bless You.

I adore You and I thank You for Your great glory and for Your goodness.

You alone are holy.

You alone are the Lord.

You alone are the Most High, Jesus Christ.

With the Holy Spirit, in the glory of God the Father.

Amen.

COMMUNION MEDITATION

Lord Jesus, Lamb of God, I am not worthy for You to come under my roof, I am not worthy for You to enter my soul, but I am still praying that You will fill me with Your presence.

Because, Lord, how can I become worthy by myself?

How can I light a lamp in my soul, Lord, if you are the Light, when You are the only one who can light up my darkness? Only You can make me see with my heart, hear with my heart, understand with my heart, so that I can sincerely repent and accept You who are the Light?

How can I heal my wounds by myself, wounds which drive me to judge and to be filled with fear? How can I heal the wounds which block me from abandoning my whole past, my present and my future, and that I totally surrender my illness to You?

How can I bring peace to my soul, when You are the only true peace?

Lord, how can my soul live if You, who are life, do not live in me?

Lord, how can my unworthy soul learn to love if You who are the

Teacher do not dwell within it?

Lord, how can I be grateful, how can I glorify You, how can I bless You, if my unworthy soul does not taste Your holy presence, if it does not feel Your peace or Your joy, if it does not experience Your redemption and healing?

Come, Lord, as my Redeemer and my Saviour, as my Doctor and Healer, come in and be the King of my heart.

Come, Jesus, say the Word and my whole being will be made whole.

Come, Jesus in me, pull me to Your cross, pull me into Your heart, because I want to give You my pains and my sickness, because I want to give You my life.

Come, Jesus, and teach me to love the way You loved us.

Amen.

PRAYING FOR THE REDEMPTION FROM THE PAIN OF WOUNDS IN THE HEART

Lord, Your Son in His body carried our pain and showed the value of weakness and suffering. Hear our prayer for our sick brothers and sisters: may they know that Christ, because of their pain and weakness, proclaims them blessed and unites their sufferings to His own for the salvation of the world. (From the collect from the Mass for the Sick)

(For feelings of rejection, unwantedness, inferiority complexes, guilt, disappointment, sadness, sorrow, depression, fear and anxiety, lack of forgiveness, hatred, and judgement. It can also be applied for those suffering from anorexia and bulimia.)

(Begin by making the sign of the cross.)

May this preparation be in the name of the Father, and of the Son, and of the Holy Spirit!

May Your grace be with me, Lord Jesus Christ, Your love, God the Father, and Your anointment, Holy Spirit.

INTENTION

Eternal Father, I offer You the sacrifice of Your Beloved Son, our Lord Jesus Christ, so that His love from the cross would redeem us from feelings of rejection and all other negative feelings, and the consequences of those feelings in our life.

THANKSGIVING

I thank You, Lord, for the gift of life.

You made me miraculously in Your likeness and image to live eternally giving me the opportunity in this short life to determine how my life would be in eternity.

In the depths of my soul, You impressed love, made me ready for sacrifice, ready to forgive, to bless and thank, ready for giving and helping.

You impressed love in me which can only be felt in You.

You received me in baptism with limitless love as Your adopted son/daughter and You invited me to discover and live that love during my life with the help of the Holy Spirit.

(Call the Holy Spirit now and remain in this prayer for as long as you feel it is necessary.)

Thank You, Lord, for choosing the time and place of my birth (mention your date of birth).

Thank You for choosing the family and the situation in life in which I was born.

(Remember your family members one by one.)

Thank You for every person in my life who was important to me.

(Remember some of them.)

Thank You for any of those who did good to me.

(Remember some of them.)

Thank You, Lord, for the angel You sent me to help me and serve me, and to help me so that I could more easily inherit salvation.

(Thank God with your heart for your guardian angel.)

Thank You for the help of the saints who willingly answer our prayers when we pray with trust for their intercession, for their help.

(Thank the saints you prayed to.)

Thank You, O Lord, for those who were an example of faith to me, who taught me about You or spoke to me about You.

(Remember some of them.)

Thank You for inspiring me to seek You and find You: in prayer, in the Sacred Scripture, in the sacraments, in religious books, in those around me who need Your mercy.

Thank You, Lord, that I often dwell in You, so that I can be filled anew with Your love, faith, peace, joy, wisdom, goodness, strength... So that I feel accepted and protected.

Thank You, my Lord, that You are ready to enter into every situation in life that I, with my whole heart, invite You into.

(Call Him now in your own words into your situation in life.)

Lord, You sent me Your Holy Spirit so that I could repeatedly be filled with His grace to enter You over and over again, and remain within You.

Lord, when I am in You, You give me grace and I can and I am willing to forgive those who, without that grace, I would be unable to forgive. You give me the grace to love, without expecting anything in return. You give me the grace that I can and I wish to undergo suffering and injustice with patience and peace.

Lord, when I am in You, You give me rest. You liberate and heal my spirit, soul, and body. You teach me and change me. You fill me with Your peace and joy.

Lord, You offer me the fullness of life, You offer me Yourself, but I often choose a different version of the fullness of life, and I place my own idols above You and above my neighbour.

Lord, when I am not with You, I become ungrateful and I often fall into sin. I try to generally justify my sin, and often my penance is not sincere.

Lord, I know that without You, without Your forgiveness, I cannot be saved.

That's why I thank You, Father, for giving us Your only Beloved Son, Jesus Christ, so that anyone who believes in Him can be saved, and can have eternal life.

Thank You, Jesus, because You, instead of me, paid the punishment for my sins and my wantonness.

Thank You because, having suffered and died on the cross, You took my sins and my wantonness.

Thank You, Lord, that You took my pain, my humiliations, my hurts and my fears on the cross.

Thank You for taking my sicknesses and healing me with Your wounds.

Thank You, Lord, for Your immeasurable love towards the downtrodden, the rejected, the sick and all other people who are suffering.

Thank You, God, for Your fatherly love for us, sinners.

Lord Jesus, You instituted the Eucharist so that in it I can always participate anew in Your redemptive passion and can access the fruits of salvation from it, and so grow in love, grace, and wisdom.

Thank You that by the Eucharist, by me receiving Your Body and Blood, I can be freed from my wantonness, from my sinful addictions, from my sinful leanings and tendencies.

Thank You for coming to me in the Eucharist by entering me as a true God and true man so that I, just like the sick and the suffering and the sinners, can receive Your grace.

REPENTANCE

First, Lord, let me bring before You my sorrow for offending You.

Lord, only You know how often I sinned thinking of others in an immature, wrong and impure way. Only You know how often I sinned by keeping silence when I should have spoken, how often I spoke words which hurt and humiliated others, how often I caused others to feel guilty, less important, rejected, and unwanted.

Forgive me, Lord.

Lord, only You know how many times I sinned by not being there when my dear ones needed me, because I failed to understand, to comfort, to protect, to praise, to hug...

(Remain in silence and remember some of your dear ones who needed you to be there for them.)

Forgive me, Lord.

(Here, name your dependency/dependencies.)

I beg You to forgive me, redeem me, and liberate me.

FORGIVENESS

Eternal Father, I offer You the sacrifice of Your dearly Beloved Son, Jesus Christ, for the redemption of my heart from its hurts and disappointments, its complexes of rejection, so that I can sincerely forgive those who have sinned against me, especially for those who caused me to feel rejected and less worthy.

Lord, only You know how many times I did not forgive those who hurt me.

Only You know how many times I did not want to, I did not know how, or I just was not able to forgive.

Forgive me, Lord.

Lord, only You know how many people felt rejected by me and how badly. I am praying for those whom I have wounded with my weaknesses, sins, and debauchery. Give them the grace to forgive me.

Please, heal their wounds. May Your peace and love make up for the pain that I have caused them.

(Try to remember those, especially among your dear ones, that you know felt rejected by you.)

Lord, You know that I really want to forgive those who sinned against me.

I want to forgive all those who I definitely know have hurt me, but also those that sinned against me that I was not even aware of it.

Lord, I want to forgive, by Your grace, really forgive those who are sorry and who repent, but also those who are not sorry that they hurt me and continue to do so.

Lord, I want to forgive all of those who were not aware that they caused me pain.

Lord, I especially care about forgiving my parents.

Lord, I know that there were situations when they were not aware that they hurt me or when they could have been better towards me, situations when they had the best of intentions, but which left deep scars in me.

I want to forgive my parents for all the situations in which I didn't feel accepted:

(try and remember some of those situations)

- situations in which I felt abandoned by them (cut off from them)
- situations in which they didn't believe me
- situations in which they didn't protect me
- situations in which they didn't praise me
- situations in which they unfairly punished me
- situations in which they failed to give me support
- situations in which they failed to communicate gentleness or intimacy

I wish to forgive my parents the situations in which I felt less worthy than my brothers or sisters.

I wish to forgive them all those times I had to watch them or hear them fighting.

I want to forgive them for the times they caused me shame and humiliation.

Lord, bring to my mind now the others who made me feel rejected and inferior.

(Remember the brothers and sisters, the grandparents, cousins and friends, teachers, spouses, children, work colleagues and bosses, people who rejected you or abused you... Forgive them now.)

Lord, I bring You the situations in which I compared myself to others, felt so inferior and I felt that You loved me less.

(Try and remember some of them.)

Lord, I bring before You all my life failures, especially those which I remember with disappointment, humiliation, and rejection.

(Try and remember some of them.)

Lord, I bring You the situations in which I felt rejected and unprotected by You, situations in which I wanted Your help, and did not receive it.

(Try and remember some of them.)

Lord, I want to give You the moments when I withdrew into self-pity, moments when I sought comfort in places which could never give it to me.

(Try to remember those situations.)

Lord, I forgive myself and everyone else that You in Your love have already forgiven. I forgive because I know that You want me to forgive.

(Try and remember some of your worst sins.)

Lord, I forgive all others too, because I want my heart to be healed and cleansed, because I want to live in Your peace. I want to taste Your love and Your joy.

Lord, I forgive all, because You created all of us and redeemed us with the same love, because You desire that all of sinners repent and live.

Jesus, You have said that we cannot do anything without You. That is why I believe that I have a foretaste of the fullness of the grace of forgiveness that's making me whole again in Communion.

I believe it begins with a loving encounter, in confession, there where You died loving me on the cross.

Lord, only You know my soul, and You know the pains which are still hurting and are unhealed and broken still.

Only You know the wounds which are still gaping and take away my joy of life.

Only You, beloved Father, know what I have pushed into my subconsciousness and is forgotten within me, but still takes away my inner joy and peace.

That is why, my God, I am asking You with Your love from the cross in this sacrifice of the Mass, redeem my feelings of rejection and its consequences on the part of those who did not know or did not want to love me.

Lord, please redeem me from my conviction of being inferior, or of my guilt complexes, redeem me from hating, from bitterness, from disappointment, from anger and rage.

Jesus, please redeem me from the need to judge and make judgements, from the need to criticise, to complain, to whine about, to speak badly about others.

Please, God, redeem me from fear and anxiety.

Please, Jesus, redeem me from self-pity and depression.

Please, Jesus, redeem me from jealousy and envy.

Please, Lord, redeem me from negative feelings and attitudes for which I am responsible.

Please, redeem me from my own negative decisions, which I have in my heart which I made trying to protect myself from further disappointment.

With Your Blood, break the power of negative words which I said to myself and the power of negative words which others spoke to me.

(You'll never be...)

Please, Lord, redeem me from the dependencies that I have that are a result of my feelings of rejection.

(Renounce these dependencies.)

Beloved Jesus, redeem me of conscious and unconscious desires to control and manipulate others.

Crucified Jesus, redeem me from my conscious and unconscious desires for recognition and acceptance, redeem me from every desire to prove myself to everyone, and grant instead that my driving force will be love for You and for my neighbour.

PROFESSION OF FAITH

Lord Jesus Christ, I firmly believe that, in Communion, I will receive Your Body and Blood, I will receive You, the Sacrificial Lamb that was humiliated, despised, rejected, inhumanely tortured, and killed for me.

I believe that You, Jesus, enter into me in Communion as a true God and true man, with Your divine and human love.

I believe that You enter in me with Your will, and I with my will want to enter You, so that in You, in Your love from the cross, I will find the strength in my soul to forgive everyone, and with faith in my heart, I will pray to the Father for all those who have wounded me.

Jesus, I believe that I enter You and You enter me, in the freedom of my heart, in total faith in Your goodness. I can hand over those scars on my soul and receive Your redemption, healing, and liberation.

Lord, I believe I will be one with You in the Eucharist. I believe I will be part of Your miraculous love from the cross.

I believe I will be filled with the Holy Spirit, and my soul which is in pain will overflow with the love of the Father.

Lord, I believe that by receiving Your body I am really bringing Your sacrifice to the Father, and I receive the grace of redemption. I receive the grace of inner healing, I receive the love of the Father, which is poured out through the Spirit, it is poured into my heart. I receive Your peace, Jesus.

And for that, Lord, I thank You from my heart.

Holy Spirit, please accompany me through this Holy Mass.

Grant that my thoughts, by Your grace, are in harmony with my words.

Grant that Your grace seizes me so completely that I can surrender myself with my whole heart to the Father's will and receive redemption.

Thank You, Holy Spirit, for helping me. Without Your grace, I do not know how to pray.

My guardian angel, protect my thoughts and my feelings during the Holy Mass so that I may be with God and in God.

Holy Mary, Mother of God, pray for me. You are the person who was most closely connected to His passion. You, who stood by the Cross, you were His comfort and strength in His hardest moments. You felt the depths of His pain, which was hidden from others.

You, Mary, together with Him, shared the pain of rejection, contempt, unwantedness, disappointment, abandonment, betrayal, shame etc.

You, like the prophet Isaiah, saw how Jesus would take our pains upon Himself, pain of the heart, soul, and body. You saw how His wounds would heal our wounds.

You, O Blessed Virgin Mary, together with Jesus, unconditionally forgave even the greatest enemies.

You, O Blessed Virgin Mother, saw and felt how pained Jesus was because of those for whom His passion would be pointless, because they wouldn't trust nor hand over their sins, pains, and sicknesses.

Holy Mary, Mother of God and my Mother, pray for me for the grace to be able to completely trust in His mercy, and receive the fullness of redemption so that Jesus', your and my joy can be complete.

Mary, I cannot offer the sacrifice of your Son, without presenting your sacrifice too. Without offering the suffering of all those who, throughout the ages, united their suffering with your Son's suffering on the cross, and my own suffering, regardless of how trivial it looks in front of yours.

May your love, Mary, reach into my soul and may your motherly love liberate me from myself so that I can completely trust in the mercy of your Son Jesus.

Pray, Mary, for the grace that I understand with even more depth the point of offering my own renunciations and sacrifices so that with increasing faith and love I can offer Jesus' sacrifice for the souls who need the grace of redemption the most.

Saint Joseph, particularly beloved by God, pray for me.

All the Saints... help me and love me in front of the throne of the Most High.

O Holy Souls in purgatory, pray for me so that I can participate in this Mass with as much fervour as possible.

Thank You, Jesus. I glorify and bless You.

I praise You, Jesus. I glorify You and bless You.

I adore You and I thank You for Your great glory and for Your goodness.

You alone are holy.

You alone are the Lord.

You alone are the Most High, Jesus Christ.

With the Holy Spirit, in the glory of God the Father.

Amen.

COMMUNION MEDITATION

Lord Jesus, Lamb of God, I am not worthy that You come under my roof, I am not worthy for You to enter my soul, but I am still praying that You will fill me with Your presence.

Because, Lord, how can I become worthy by myself?

How can I light a lamp in my soul Lord, if You are the Light, when You are the only one who can light up my darkness? Only You can make me see with my heart, hear with my heart, understand with my heart, so that I can sincerely repent and accept You who are the Light?

How can I heal my wounds by myself, wounds which drive me to judge and to be filled with fear? How can I heal the wounds which block me from surrendering my whole past, my present, and my future, and totally surrender my illness to You?

How can I bring peace to my soul, when You are the only true peace?

Lord, how can my soul live if You, who are Life, do not live in it?

Lord, how can my unworthy soul love if You, who are the Teacher, do not dwell within it?

Lord, how can I be grateful, how can I glorify You, how can I bless You if my unworthy soul does not taste Your holy presence, if it does not taste Your peace nor Your joy?

Come, Lord, as my Redeemer and my Saviour, as my Doctor and Healer, come in and be the King of my heart.

Come, Jesus, say the Word and my whole being will be made whole.

Come, Jesus, in me, attract me to Your cross, pull me into Your heart, because I want to hand over my pain, because I want to give You my wounded heart.

Come, Jesus, and teach me to love the way You love us.

Amen.

PRAYING FOR **REPARATION OF DAMAGES, THE PENANCE**

Lord, have mercy on us by the suffering of Your Son. By our deeds, we do not deserve this, but we have recourse to Your mercy and unique sacrifice of Jesus Christ, who reigns with You. (Offertory, Palm Sunday Liturgy)

WITH OUR THOUGHTS, WORDS, AND deeds, and by omitting to do good when we could have, we have hurt many people. Whether we are conscious of it or not, we have encouraged others to sin, and with others we have sinned together. Sincere repentance, confession, and penances (which are irreplaceable) can turn a lot of things to good.

(Begin with the sign of the cross.)

May this preparation be in the name of the Father, and of the Son, and of the Holy Spirit!

May Your grace be with me, Lord Jesus Christ, Your love, God my Father, and Your anointing, Holy Spirit.

INTENTION

Eternal Father, I offer You the sacrifice of Your dearly Beloved Son, Jesus Christ, for all of those who I wounded with my sins, all of those with whom I sinned, and for those who I either consciously or unconsciously led into sin.

THANKSGIVING

Lord Jesus Christ, I thank You that, with Your passion and death, You redeemed us from sin and from the consequences of sin.

I thank You for taking on Yourself our pain and our sicknesses.

I thank You for healing our wounds.

Thank You, Lord, that You take every sin upon Yourself, that You forgive every sin that we hand over to You with sorrow and regret, with trust in Your mercy.

I thank You, Lord, that You redeem us, that You take every pain which we give to You with trust in Your love.

Thank You, Jesus, that You heal all wounds of the heart that we hand over to You with faith in Your goodness.

Thank You, our God, that You constantly draw us to Yourself, that You want us to come to You whenever we are weary or burdened, every time we are wounded, and every time we see that, by our sins, we have hurt You or our neighbour.

Thank You, Lord, because only in Your presence can we sufficiently repent, and only in Your presence can we hope to receive Your forgiveness.

Thank You, Lord, that in Your presence we can pray with faith for those whom we have wounded. Only in Your presence can we trust in Your goodness that You will heal the hearts of those who we have hurt, and You can give back whatever we have damaged and broken.

Thank You, Lord, because only in Your presence can we sincerely, with our hearts, forgive those who have sinned against us.

Thank You, Jesus, because only You can give in our hearts true peace and true joy.

REPENTANCE

Today, Lord, in front of Your cross, I wish to put all those whom I wounded with my thoughts, words, deeds, and sins of omission.

(Take enough time, examine your conscience, and trusting in the help of the Holy Spirit, bring to Jesus the people that you wounded with your sins.)

Lord, You make reparation to them.

Draw them to Yourself, give them rest, take their pain, and heal their wounds.

Lord Jesus, Saviour and our Redeemer, I bring all of those with whom I sinned, and, of course, all of those whom I led into sin.

(Take enough time, examine your conscience, and trusting in the help of the Holy Spirit, bring to Jesus the people with whom you sinned or those that you inspired to commit sin.)

I ask You, Lord, to forgive us and heal our wounds.

I ask You to draw us closer to Yourself, to Your love on the cross.

PLEA

Grant me, Lord, the grace that I am often inspired to offer Your sacrifice to the Father for those whom I have hurt with my sins.

Grant, Lord, the grace that I often pray, that I often offer Your sacrifice to the Father for those with whom I sinned and those whom I consciously or unconsciously led to sin.

Inflame my heart with a love for them. Grant by Your grace that that love is expressed by offering Your sacrifice for their redemption, their healing, their conversion, and consecration.

You, Lord, in Your love, turn all the ill I did to them into their eternal good.

(Once more, remember some of those people and bring them before the Lord.)

HOLY MASS

Lord, I believe that in the Mass I will hear Your Word. I believe that You will speak to me. I believe You will teach me, comfort me, and encourage me. I believe that You will illuminate my conscience.

Lord, I believe that You will draw me to Yourself throughout the whole Mass.

I believe that You want my heart and my words to be focused on You. I believe that You want me to immerse my whole being in You.

My Jesus, I believe that You want me to experience Your peace, Your goodness, Your closeness, Your care for me. I believe that You want me to feel Your holy presence at this Mass.

Lord Jesus Christ, my Saviour and Redeemer, I firmly believe that in this Communion I will receive You, the Sacrificial Lamb that was killed for us.

I believe that You, Jesus, come into me in Communion as true God and true man with Your divine and human love.

I believe that this Communion, in which You are in me and I am in

You, is the centre of my life.

I want to concentrate all my attention on You at that moment, I want to love You with my whole being, I want to completely surrender myself to Your goodness and Your love.

I want to embrace You on Your cross, Jesus, and to hand over all those for whom I offer this sacrifice to the Father.

(Remember some of them.)

Jesus, I want, while loving You in those moments, to learn to love my neighbour.

My God, I want to thank You, I want to thank and glorify You.

I want to rejoice, because You turn everything into good for those who love You.

Lord, I want to enjoy Your presence.

I bless You, Lord. I bless Your grace, which I will experience in the Mass which I will offer to the Father for all those people that, by Your grace, I care about.

I thank You, because in every Holy Mass, You change me. Thank You for multiplying my faith so that I can pray with true trust in Your response. Thank You for strengthening my hope in Your goodness.

I thank You for teaching me to love the way You loved.

INTERCESSION

O Holy Mary, Mother of Jesus, Queen of Peace, pray for me.

You, Mary, are the one who is most deeply connected to Jesus' passion and death. You stood by the cross, you were His comfort and strength in His hardest moments. You felt the depths of His pain, which was hidden from others.

You, like the prophet Isaiah, could see Jesus taking our sins upon Himself. You saw how He took our sins, pains, and sicknesses. You could see how His wounds heal us.

Mary, you saw and felt Jesus' pain for those for whom His passion and death would be pointless, because they would not trust, nor hand over their sins, pains, and sicknesses.

Holy Mary, Mother of God and my Mother, pray for all of those whom I have hurt (name some of them) for the grace to be able to completely trust in Jesus' mercy, and receive the fullness of redemption, so that Jesus', your and my joy can be complete.

Mary, I cannot offer the sacrifice of your Son without presenting your sacrifice too, and the suffering of all those who, throughout the ages, united their suffering with your Son's suffering on the cross. I cannot offer it without offering my own suffering, regardless of how trivial it might look compared with yours and His.

Holy Mary, Mother of God, bring Your dying Son to those whose redemption I'm offering His sacrifice to the Father for.

May your love, Mary, come deeply into their souls to those parts which are unable to reject your motherly love.

May your love, Mary, draw them to your Son Jesus, so that they can trust in His mercy, call out His name and completely hand over their pain, especially the pain that I caused.

Pray, Mary, for the grace that I understand with even more depth the point of offering my own renunciations and sacrifices, so that with increasing faith and love I can offer Jesus' sacrifice for the souls who need the grace of redemption the most.

Saint Joseph, dearly loved by God, pray for us.

Mother Mary and Saint Joseph, pray for us, sinners, pray for me and for those whom I wounded with my sins, for those with whom I committed sin, and those who I consciously or unconsciously influenced to commit sin.

O saints of God, pray for us.

(Continue with the prayer to the saints whose intercession you usually ask.)

COMMUNION MEDITATION

Lord, I know that I am not worthy that You should enter under my roof, and yet I ask You with my whole heart that You will fill me with Your presence.

Because, my Jesus, how can I ever become worthy by myself?

How can I light the light in this soul by myself if You alone are the light, if You alone are the only one that can light up my darkness, so that I can see with my heart, understand with my heart – that I sincerely repent and receive the Light?

How can I, without You, my Saviour, give peace to my own soul if You alone are Peace?

How can my soul live if You, who are Life, are not dwelling within?

How can my soul learn to love if the Teacher, who is Love, is not dwelling within?

Lord, how can I be thankful, how will I glorify You, how will I bless You, if my unworthy soul does not taste Your presence, if it does not experience Your peace and Your joy?

Enter, Lord, my soul with Your salvation and Your redemption as my Teacher and be King of my heart.

Enter, Jesus, say the Word and my whole being will be healed.

Enter, Jesus, and pull me to Your cross, pull me into Your heart, because I want to give You my pain, because I want to hand over my wounded heart.

Enter, Jesus, and teach me to love the way You loved.

Enter, Jesus, because I, together with You and with Your love, want to pray to the Father to have mercy on those who I am bringing to You in this Mass.

THE STRUCTURE OF THE MASS

The order of the Mass is made up of two main parts: the liturgy of the Word and the Eucharistic liturgy (CCC 1346), and the entrance and concluding rites.

A) The Introductory Rite

1. Entrance Hymn, Introductory Words,

2. Sign of the Cross, Greeting,

3. Penitential Act

4. The Gloria

5. Collect

B) The Liturgy of the Word

1. The readings 1st and 2nd Reading and the Psalm in-between.

2. The Gospel

3. The homily

4. The Creed

5. Prayers of the faithful

C) The Liturgy of the Eucharist

1. The preparation of the Gifts with Preparatory Prayers

2. Prayers over the Offerings (Preface)

3. The Eucharistic prayer

4. The Rite of Communion

   • The Lord's Prayer - Our Father
   • The Rite of Peace
   • The Breaking of the Bread
   • The Invitation to Communion Prayer

D) The Concluding Rite

1. Announcements

2. Blessing

3. Dismissal

THE INTRODUCTORY RITE

Remark:

In the places where it is recommended that we can add our own thoughts, I have put the letter (M)

In the places where I have added my own commentary, I have put the symbol (C)

ENTRANCE INTO THE CHURCH

When the people gather and the priest and others officiating arrive at the altar, an entrance hymn is usually sung at this time.

(C) We should be there well before this so that we can prepare our hearts for an active and efficacious participation in redemption.

GREETING, ENTRANCE HYMN, AND INTRODUCTORY WORDS

Arriving at the altar, the priest and his servers demonstrate the appropriate honour by kissing the altar, and, if suitable, by using incense. The servers then go to their seats.

When the entrance hymn is over, the priest and the faithful, still standing, make the sign of the cross, and the priest says:

In the name of the Father, and of the Son, and of the Holy Spirit.

(C) We become aware that we will encounter all three of the divine persons during the Mass and we will have to draw our attention to the person we are addressing. How can we direct our attention to the very person we are communicating in prayer if we are not aware who that person is?!

The congregation replies

Amen.

After this, the priest, turned towards the people, opens his arms and says one of the three formulas:

1. *The grace of the Lord Jesus Christ, the love of the Father, and the fellowship of the Holy Spirit be with you all.*

2. *May Grace and peace be with you from God, our Father, and our Lord Jesus Christ.*

3. *The Lord be with you.*

C) These greetings are words that we should often meditate on, but also use in everyday life, in our encounters with people with the intention that we meditate in what that greeting communicates. If, for whatever reason, we are unable to say them aloud, we should say them in our hearts.

The congregation replies:

> *And with your spirit.*

When it is the bishop who offers the Mass, he greets by saying:

> *Peace be with you.*

The priest or the deacon, or whoever else is officiating, can begin the Mass after the greeting with the opening words or with the words of the opening hymn:

> *Have mercy on me, Lord, for I am faint;*
> *heal me for my bones are in agony.*

(C) The entrance hymn is from the rite for the Mass for the Sick.

ACT OF CONTRITION

After this, the Act of Contrition follows. The priest leads the faithful in the words of penance:

> *Brethren (brothers and sisters), let us acknowledge our sins,*
> *and so prepare ourselves to celebrate the sacred mysteries.*

Or

> *Brothers and sisters, to begin to celebrate the memory of the Lord,*
> *let us examine our conscience and admit that we are sinful people.*

Or

> *Brothers and sisters, we gather to listen to the Word of God and to celebrate the sacrifice of Christ, and so we will prepare and ask God to forgive us our sins.*

Or

> *Brothers and sisters, in order to worthily celebrate the memory of the Lord, let us each examine ourselves, admit our guilt before God and the Church and forgive each other our sins.*

Or

> *Brothers and sisters, at the beginning of this mass celebration, let us compose ourselves and ask for the mercy of the Lord.*

After a short pause, the act of penitence is said, and the priest can choose among three ways.

(C) That pause in silence is absolutely necessary in order to remember or call to mind the examination of conscience that we did before the Mass.

THE FIRST WAY

All confess together:

> *I confess to almighty God, and to you, my brothers and sisters, that I have sinned through my own fault, in my thoughts and in my words, in what I have done, and in what I have failed to do;*

and beating our breasts we say:

> *through my fault, my fault, my most grievous fault.*

(C) All of us have sins or weaknesses which overpower us at times. We become aware of our sinfulness, that is, of sins which, without the grace of God, we cannot conquer. That is why we pray for liberation or for the strength to resist them. Whoever thinks he/she is without such sin is lying to themselves.

And so we continue:

> *and I ask blessed Mary, ever virgin, all the angels and saints, and
> you, my brothers and sisters, to pray for me to the Lord our God. (M)*

THE SECOND WAY

The priest says:

> *Have mercy on us, O Lord.*

The congregation answers:

> *Because we have sinned against you. (M)*

The priest:

> *Show unto us Your mercy, O Lord.*

The congregation:

> *And grant us Your salvation. (M)*

· The third way:

After a short silence, the priest or the concelebrant says the following or
some other invocation with *Lord, have mercy:*

> *O Lord, you were sent to heal the brokenhearted, have mercy on us.*

The congregation answers:

> *Lord, have mercy. (M)*

The priest:

> *Christ, who came to call sinners, have mercy on us.*

The congregation:

> *Christ, have mercy. (M)*

The priest:

> *Lord, who sits at the right hand of the Father to intercede for us, have mercy on us.*

The congregation:

> *Lord, have mercy. (M)*

After one of the three ways of confessing, the priest's absolution follows:

> *May Almighty God have mercy on us,*
> *forgive us our sins,*
> *and bring us all to everlasting life.*

The congregation answers:

> *Amen.*

LORD, HAVE MERCY

The *Lord, have mercy* invocation follows, which might be preceded by some form of introductory for this penitential prayer.

> *Lord, have mercy*
> *Lord, have mercy (M)*
>
> *Christ, have mercy*
> *Christ, have mercy (M)*
>
> *Lord, have mercy*
> *Lord, have mercy (M)*

(C) During these invocations, we bring our intentions. We allow the Spirit to inspire us both for our needs and for the needs of others.

GLORY TO GOD IN THE HIGHEST

After this, when it is announced, we sing or we say the melodious *Glory*:

C) *The* Glory *is one of the most perfect prayers existing. Let us try to pray it with as much care as possible.*

> *Glory to God in the highest,*
> *and on earth peace to people of good will.*
>
> *We praise You,*
> *we bless You,*
> *we adore You,*
> *we glorify You,*
> *we give You thanks for Your great glory,*
> *Lord God, heavenly King,*
> *O God, Almighty Father.*
>
> *Lord Jesus Christ, only Begotten Son,*
> *Lord God, Lamb of God, Son of the Father,*
> *You take away the sins of the world,*
> *have mercy on us; (M)*
> *You take away the sins of the world,*
> *receive our prayer; (M)*
> *You are seated at the right hand of the Father,*
> *have mercy on us. (M)*
>
> *For You alone are the Holy One,*
> *You alone are the Lord,*
> *You alone are the Most High,*
> *Jesus Christ,*
> *with the Holy Spirit,*
> *in the glory of God the Father.*
> *Amen.*

THE COLLECT PRAYER

When the *Gloria* is finished, the priest with joined hands says:

Let us pray.

Altogether we pray in silence with the priest and then the priest with extended hands prays the collect prayers. He can choose one of two:

> *Almighty God, Your Son carried our pain in His flesh and showed the value of weakness and suffering. Hear our prayer for our sick brothers and sisters: let the recognition that, by their pains and weaknesses, Christ proclaims them blessed and unites His sufferings to theirs for the salvation of the world.*

Or:

> *Almighty and eternal God, salvation of all believers! We call on Your mercy for our sick: may they return to health and grant that they thank You in Your Church.*

C) These examples of the collect are taken from the Mass for the Sick. It is important to understand the collect prayer (so that we are conscious of which of the divine persons we are addressing). Otherwise, we cannot pray neither with our minds nor our hearts. The short silence here is very necessary, in which we can understand with our minds and will in our hearts the content of the Collect. It is imperative to reflect and honour every Mass prayer (giving it special attention).

The Collect concludes in one of three following ways. (In the Mass for the Sick, only the first example applies.)

> *Through our Lord, Jesus Christ, Your Son, who lives and reigns with You and the Holy Spirit, one God, forever and ever.*

Or

> *You live and reign with God the Father in the unity of the Holy Spirit, one God, forever and ever.*

Or

Who lives and reigns with You and the Holy spirit, one God, forever and ever.

The congregation answers:

Amen.

THE LITURGY OF THE WORD

FIRST READING

After this, a reader will go to the lectern and read the first reading which everyone sits down to listen to.

2 Kings 20:1-6

I have seen your tears, I will heal you.

A reading from the Second book of Kings

In those days, Hezekiah became sick and was at the point of death. The prophet Isaiah son of Amoz came to him, and said to him, "Thus says the Lord: Set your house in order, for you shall die; you shall not recover." Then Hezekiah turned his face to the wall and prayed to the Lord: "Remember now, O, Lord, I implore you, how I have walked before you in faithfulness with a whole heart, and have done what is good in your sight." Hezekiah wept bitterly.

Before Isaiah had gone out of the middle court, the word of the Lord came to him: "Turn back, and say to Hezekiah prince of my people, Thus says the Lord, the God of your ancestor David: I have heard your prayer, I have seen your tears; indeed, I will heal you; on the third day you shall go up to the house of the Lord. I will add fifteen years to your life. I will deliver you and this city out of the hand of the king of Assyria; I will defend this city for my own sake and for my servant David's sake.

(C) The reading is taken from the Lectionary for the Mass for the Sick. What is important is that we hear the whole content of the text. But, at the same time, we should be attentive because God can sometimes personally speak to us in the way that some of the text will "stand out from" the rest.

As a signal that the reading is finished, the reader proclaims:

This is the Word of the Lord.

The congregation replies:

Thanks be to God.

C) If we are not grateful to God for His Word, if that "Thanks be to God" is not sincere, if it doesn't come from the understanding and the heart, we must ask ourselves if we love Him (Jn. 14:23-4).

PSALM

The psalmist or the cantor leads the psalm, and the congregation sings or repeats the chorus responsorial verse.

Is. 38:10-12 and 16 R cf v.17

R: You have held back my life from the pit of doom, O Lord.

I said, "In the prime of my life
must I go through the gates of death
and be robbed of the rest of my years?" R

I said, "I will not again see the Lord himself
in the land of the living;
no longer will I look on my fellow man,
or be with those who now dwell in this world. R

Like a shepherd's tent my house
has been pulled down and taken from me.
Like a weaver I have rolled up my life,
and he has cut me off from the loom;
day to night you made an end of me; R

For you, Lord, my heart will live
you gave me back my spirit;
you cured me, kept me alive,
changed my sickness into health. R

(C) This psalm is taken from the rite of the Mass for the Sick.

SECOND READING

After this, if another reading is to be read, the reader goes to the lectern as above.

Acts 28:7-10

The sick people on the Island came to Paul and were cured.

A reading from the Acts of the Apostles.

Now in the neighbourhood of that place were lands belonging to the leading man of the island, named Publius, who received us and entertained us hospitably for three days. It so happened that the father of Publius lay sick in bed with fever and dysentery. Paul visited him and cured him by praying and putting his hands on him. After this happened, the rest of the people on the island who had diseases also came and were cured. They bestowed many honours to us; and when we were about to sail, they put on board all the provisions we needed.

(C) The reading is taken from the Mass for the Sick.

As a sign that the reading is finished, the reader proclaims:

This is the Word of the Lord.

The congregation replies:

Thanks be to God.

THE GOSPEL

The *Alleluia* follows or another song.

Mt. 8:17
(Alleluia)

He took our sicknesses away
and carried our diseases for us.

At this point, the deacon who has to announce the Gospel bows before the priest and whispers seeking a blessing:

Lord, give me a blessing.

The priest says softly:

May the Lord be in your heart and on your lips:
that you may worthily proclaim His Gospel:
in the name of the Father, and of the Son, and of the Holy Spirit.

(C) All the readings should be read in a dignified and appropriate manner, that is with understanding so that the listeners can hear and understand. More than reading a text the reader should proclaim the Word because it is a "living" word, it is God's message for today; therefore it is ideal that a reader prepares the readings in a prayerful manner before.

The deacon answers:

Amen.

If there is no deacon, the priest bows before the altar and softly says:

Almighty God, cleanse my heart and my lips that I may worthily proclaim Your holy Gospel.

At this point, the deacon or the priest goes to the pulpit and says:

The Lord be with you.

The congregation answers:

And with your spirit.

The deacon or the priest:

A reading from the Holy Gospel according to X.

Before this, he makes the sign of the cross on his forehead, his lips, and his chest.

The congregation responds:

Glory to you, O Lord.

The deacon or the priest read the Gospel

Mt. 8:14-17

He took our sicknesses away.

A reading from the Holy Gospel according to Matthew.

When Jesus entered Peter's house, he saw his mother-in-law lying in bed with a fever; he touched her hand, and the fever left her, and she got up and began to serve him. That evening they brought to him many who were possessed with demons; and he cast out the spirits with a word, and cured all who were sick. This was to fulfill what had been spoken through the prophet Isaiah, "He took our infirmities and bore our diseases."

(C) The Gospel is taken from the Mass for the Sick.

When the Gospel ends, the deacon or priest says:

This is the Word of the Lord.

All acclaim:

Glory to you, O Lord.

Then the priest or the deacon kisses the book and quietly says:

By the words of the Gospel, may our sins be wiped out.

(C) Here we can understand the prayer like this: "Grant, Lord, that Your Word enters our hearts and enlightens us to our sins and gives us a true love of Jesus in order to repent sincerely."

THE HOMILY

The sermon follows, which is normal for Sundays and feast-days, but is recommended also for other days.

(C) When the homily comes from a priest's meditations on the Mass readings, it is a gift of God to the faithful gathered at Mass which will have a great impact on the hearers.. When the homily is only the result of the priest's thoughts about the readings, then it is just a teaching which may be less effective.

A short pause after the homily is always good for the faithful to be able to recall the most important things they heard.

After the homily, at the appropriate time, we profess our faith.

THE CREED

(C) At this point, many of the faithful are losing concentration, and the Creed is often said in an "automatic" fashion, so they do not participate in it with understanding and from the heart. It is good to exchange the first three words "I believe in" in our thoughts with, for instance, "I trust in" or "I have confidence in." In that way, we give full meaning to the Creed.

I believe in one God,
the Father Almighty,
maker of Heaven and earth,
of all things visible and invisible.

I believe in one Lord Jesus Christ,
the only Begotten Son of God,
born of the Father before all age
God from God, Light from Light,
true God from true God,
begotten, not made, consubstantial with the Father;
through Him all things were made.
For us men and for our salvation
He came down from Heaven,
and by the Holy Spirit was incarnate of the Virgin Mary,

At the words that follow up to and including

and became man,
all bow.

For our sake He was crucified under Pontius Pilate,
He suffered death and was buried,
and rose again on the third day
in accordance with the Scriptures.
He ascended into Heaven
and is seated at the right hand of the Father.
He will come again in
to judge the living and the dead
and His kingdom will have no end.

I believe in the Holy Spirit, the Lord, the giver of life,
who proceeds from the Father and the Son,
who with the Father and the Son is adored and glorified,
who has spoken through the prophets.

I believe in one, holy, Catholic and apostolic Church.
I confess one baptism for the forgiveness of sins
and I look forward to the resurrection of the dead
and the life of the world to come. Amen.

THE PRAYERS OF THE FAITHFUL

(C) After every pronounced prayer, before the faithful utter the response "Lord, hear our prayer" or something similar, it is good to spend a few seconds in silence. In silence, we can understand and accept what we are praying for so that our prayers are not just said with our lips but with the involvement of our hearts and minds. After the reading of the prayers, the priest leaves a moment's silence so that the faithful can add their own prayers in their hearts.

THE LITURGY OF THE EUCHARIST

THE PREPARATION OF THE GIFTS

After this, the offertory hymn begins. The servers put the corporal, the chalice, the Missal, and the purifier on the altar.

It is desirable that the faithful participate in the offertory by bringing up the bread or the wine for the celebration of the Eucharist, or other gifts which are for the needs of the Church or the poor.

The priest standing at the altar takes the paten with the bread and, holding it a little above the altar, quietly says:

Blessed are You, Lord God of all creation,
for through Your goodness we have received
the bread we offer You:
fruit of the earth and work of human hands,
it will become for us the bread of life.

If we do not sing the offertory, then the priest says it aloud, and the faithful reply with the acclamation:

(C) Ideally, at the time of the preparation of the gifts, it is good to prepare our intentions in our heart and to accept the will of God. This is also the time in which we offer to God our family, other people we are praying for, our work, and other intentions that are on our mind, and we should especially remember here the souls in purgatory.

> *Blessed be God forever*

The deacon or the priest pours wine and water into a chalice and quietly says:

> *By the mystery of this water and wine*
> *may we come to share in the divinity of Christ*
> *who humbled himself to share in our humanity.*

After this the priest quietly says:

> *Blessed are You, Lord God of all creation,*
> *for through Your goodness we have received*
> *the wine we offer You:*
> *fruit of the vine and work of human hands,*
> *it will become our spiritual drink.*

If the offertory chant is not sung, the priest may speak these words aloud. At the end, the congregation may acclaim:

> *Blessed be God forever*

After this, the priest, bowing profoundly, says quietly:

> *With humble spirit and contrite heart*
> *may we be accepted by You, O Lord,*
> *and may our sacrifice in Your sight this day*
> *be pleasing to You, Lord God.*

(C) If, at Mass, we are in front of God and we have come without faith, love, humility and contrition, and we are asking for the redemption of someone else, how can our prayer be pleasing to God?

The priest then, standing at the side of the altar, washes his hands saying:

> *Wash me, O Lord, from my iniquity*
> *and cleanse me from my sin.*

Standing at the middle of the altar, facing the people, extending and then joining his hands, he says:

> *Pray, brothers and sisters*
> *that my sacrifice and yours*
> *may be acceptable to God,*
> *the Almighty Father.*

(C) Let us become aware for whom we are offering this mass, both the priest and ourselves personally.

The congregation says:

> *May the Lord accept the sacrifice at your hands*
> *for the praise and glory of His name,*
> *for our good*
> *and the good of all His holy Church.*

THE OFFERTORY PRAYER

Then the priest, with hands extended, says the prayer over the offerings, at the end of which the congregation acclaims:

> *God, in whose hands are all the moments of our lives.*
> *Accept our prayers and offerings and have mercy on our brothers and sisters who are ill:*
> *Hold back the dangers which threaten them and grant that we may rejoice in their healing, through Christ our Lord.*

(C) *This offertory prayer is from the rite of the Mass for the Sick.*

Amen.

THE EUCHARISTIC PRAYER

(C) *The second and third Eucharistic prayers are the ones most often used. Here, I will just present the second.*

The priest begins the Eucharistic prayer. Opening his arms, he says:

The Lord be with you.

The congregation answers:

And with your spirit.

(C) *We can understand it like this: "May the Lord (we want this both for ourselves and for the priest) be in our thoughts, may all our attention be focused on Him."*

The priest says:

Lift up your hearts.

(C) *We can understand it like this: "Let us become conscious of God and His glory in Heaven. May our heart and all our attention be focused on His heavenly glory." A good meditation/preparation for this is to read the Book of Revelations which describes God's greatness, glory, and power.*

The congregation says:

We lift them up to the Lord.

The priest says:

Let us give thanks to the Lord our God.

The congregation:

It is right and just.

(C) We often discover the true meaning of these words when we are in some sort of trouble from which only God can deliver us, or when we find ourselves facing death, conscious that we will stand before God's judgement. Which is why we are asking God to give us His grace so that we come to know their meaning as soon as possible, and not to wait till the hour of our death.

The priest:

It is truly right and just, our duty and our salvation,
always and everywhere to give You thanks, Father Most Holy,
through Your Beloved Son, Jesus Christ,
Your Word through whom You made all things,
whom You sent as our Saviour and Redeemer,
incarnate by the Holy Spirit and born of the Virgin.
Fulfilling Your will and gaining for You a holy people,
He stretched out His hands as He endured His Passion,
so as to break the bonds of death and manifest the resurrection.
And so, with the Angels and all the Saints
we declare Your glory,
as with one voice we acclaim:

All:

Holy, Holy, Holy, Lord God of hosts.
Heaven and earth are full of Your glory.
Hosanna in the highest.
Blessed is He who comes in the name of the Lord.
Hosanna in the highest.

(C) Jesus is the one who will come in the name of the Lord. That is why we will bless Him and glorify Him, and focus all our attention on His coming to the altar among us, we acclaim Him. He comes as a true God and true man. He is King of King and Lord of Lords, but He is also the Sacrificed Lamb who gives Himself up right at this moment.

The priest, with hands held out, says:

You are indeed Holy, O Lord,
the fount of all holiness.

(C) We remind ourselves that the priest is addressing the Father in our name as well as his own.

Then he joins his hands and holding them open over the gifts says:

Make holy, therefore, these gifts, we pray,
by sending down Your Spirit upon them like the dewfall,
Then he joins them and makes the sign of the cross over the bread
and the chalice saying:
so that they may become for us
the Body and Blood of our Lord Jesus Christ.

He joins his hands again, takes the bread and holding it a little above the altar continues:

At the time He was betrayed
and entered willingly into His Passion,
He took bread and, giving thanks, broke it,
and gave it to His disciples, saying:

(C) Without gratitude, we cannot have an intimate personal relationship with God. Jesus was grateful to His Father in everything. St. Paul encourages us always and everywhere to be thankful. Preparation for the Mass begins with gratitude, and that is how every one of our prayers should begin. Gratitude and thanksgiving need to be our basic attitude if we are true believers.

The priest bows slightly and says:

TAKE THIS, ALL OF YOU,
AND EAT OF IT,
FOR THIS IS MY BODY,
WHICH WILL BE GIVEN UP FOR YOU.

He elevates the consecrated host to the people, puts it back down on the paten, genuflects, and bows.

Then he continues:

In a similar way, when supper was ended,
He took the chalice

He takes the chalice in his hands and holding it slightly above the altar, says:

and, once more giving thanks,
He gave it to His disciples, saying

He bows a little

TAKE THIS, ALL OF YOU, AND DRINK FROM IT,
FOR THIS IS THE CHALICE OF MY BLOOD,
THE BLOOD OF THE NEW AND ETERNAL COVENANT,
WHICH WILL BE POURED OUT FOR YOU AND FOR MANY
FOR THE FORGIVENESS OF SINS.
DO THIS IN MEMORY OF ME.

He elevates the chalice to the congregation, puts it on the corporal, genuflects, and bows.

He then proclaims:

The mystery of faith:

And the congregation answers with the acclamation:

1. We proclaim Your Death, O Lord,
and profess Your Resurrection
until You come again.

(C) Here we are participating in Jesus' death and resurrection on Calvary: at each consecration the same one sacrifice of Jesus on the Cross is "re-presented" for us today for our active redemption. But this Mystery also incorporates His Resurrection, His rising from the death, and His glorious return is not

something that we are only waiting for at the end of time, but already in every Holy Mass, and especially in the Consecration and receiving Holy Communion. That awaiting Jesus on the altar, and then in our hearts, is the most important reason that we come to Mass. Glorifying Jesus' resurrection, we become conscious of our own desire to rise, and we rejoice ahead of time for this. If we have not learned to joyfully await Him in Communion, how can we expect to joyfully await His second coming, how can we rejoice in the idea of Heaven?

> *2. When we eat this Bread and drink this Cup,*
> *we proclaim Your Death, O Lord,*
> *until You come again.*

Or:

> *Save us, Saviour of the world,*
> *for by Your Cross and Resurrection*
> *You have set us free.*

And so the priest with outstretched hands says:

> *Therefore, as we celebrate*
> *the memorial of His Death and Resurrection,*
> *we offer You, Lord,*
> *the Bread of life and the Chalice of salvation,*
> *giving thanks that You have held us worthy*
> *to be in Your presence and minister to You.*
> *Humbly we pray that,*
>
> *partaking of the Body and Blood of Christ,*
> *we may be gathered into one by the Holy Spirit.*
> *Remember, Lord, Your Church,*
> *spread throughout the world,*
> *and bring her to the fullness of charity,*
> *together with N., our Pope, and N., our Bishop**
> *and all the clergy.*

At the Masses for the Dead we can add:

> *Remember Your servant N.,*
> *whom You have called (today)*
> *from this world to Yourself.*
> *Grant that he (she) who was united with Your Son in baptism,*
> *may also be one with him in His Resurrection.*
> *Remember also our brothers and sisters*
> *who have fallen asleep in the hope of the Resurrection,*
>
> *and all who have died in Your mercy*
> *welcome them into the light of Your face.*
> *Have mercy on us all, we pray,*
> *that with the Blessed Virgin Mary, Mother of God,*
> *with the blessed Apostles,*
> *and all the Saints who have pleased You throughout the ages,*
> *we may merit to be coheirs to eternal life,*
> *and may praise and glorify You*

He joins his hands saying:

> *through Your Son, Jesus Christ.*
> *He takes the paten with the host and the chalice, raises them both*
> *and says:*

> *THROUGH HIM, WITH HIM, IN HIM,*
> *IN THE UNITY OF THE HOLY SPIRIT,*
> *ALL GLORY AND HONOUR IS YOURS,*
> *ALMIGHTY FATHER,*
> *FOR EVER AND EVER*

and the congregation acclaims

> *Amen.*

COMMUNION RITE

THE LORD'S PRAYER

Leaving down the chalice and paten, the priest with joined hands says:

Instructed by thy saving precepts, and following Thy divine institution, we dare to say:

Or

*At the Saviour's command
and formed by divine teaching,
we dare to say:*

Or

Let us pray as the Lord Himself taught us:

Or

We are called the children of God, so full of trust we pray:

With open hands and together with the people he prays:

*Our Father, who art in Heaven,
hallowed be Thy name;
Thy kingdom come, (M)
Thy will be done
on earth as it is in Heaven. (M)
Give us this day our daily bread, (M)
and forgive us our trespasses, (M)
as we forgive those who trespass against us; (M)
and lead us not into temptation, (M)
but deliver us from evil. (M)*

The priest continues with outstretched hands:

Deliver us, Lord, we pray, from every evil,
graciously grant peace in our days, (M)
that, by the help of Your mercy,
we may be always free from sin (M)
and safe from all distress, (M)
as we await the blessed hope
and the coming of our Saviour, Jesus Christ.

(This prayer "Deliver us, Lord, we pray, from every evil " is a very powerful prayer against evil spirits, spiritual warfare attacks and sinful addictions and should be prayed with faith, and conviction that the Lord will help the person praying for freedom from such attacks and addictions)C

He joins his hands.

The congregation says the acclamation:

For the kingdom,
the power and the glory
are Yours now and forever.

THE SIGN OF PEACE

After this, the priest with extended hands says:

Lord Jesus Christ,
who said to Your Apostles;
Peace I leave you, my peace I give you;
look not on our sins,
but on the faith of Your Church,
and graciously grant her peace and unity
in accordance with Your will.

He joins his hands and says:

Who lives and reigns for ever and ever.

The congregation answers:

Amen.

The priest stretches out his hands and closes them again saying:

The peace of the Lord be with you always.

The congregation replies:

And with your spirit.

If appropriate, the deacon or the priest adds:

Let us offer each other the sign of peace.

The congregation turns to those near them and shakes hands or hugs them or shows some other appropriate gesture.

THE BREAKING OF THE BREAD AND COMMUNION

The priest then takes the host, breaks it over the paten, and places a small piece in the chalice, saying quietly:

May this mingling of the Body and Blood
of our Lord Jesus Christ
bring eternal life to us who receive it.

At this time, Lamb of God is either sung or said:

Lamb of God, You take away the sins of the world,
have mercy on us. (M)
Lamb of God, You take away the sins of the world,
have mercy on us. (M)
Lamb of God, You take away the sins of the world,
grant us peace. (M)

Then the priest with joined hands says:

> *Lord Jesus Christ, Son of the living God,*
> *who, by the will of the Father*
> *and the work of the Holy Spirit,*
> *through Your Death gave life to the world,*
> *free me by this, Your most holy Body and Blood,*
> *from all my sins and from every evil;*
> *keep me always faithful to Your commandments,*
> *and never let me be parted from You.*

Or:

> *May the receiving of Your Body and Blood,*
> *Lord Jesus Christ,*
> *not bring me to judgement and condemnation,*
> *but through Your loving mercy*
> *be for me protection in mind and body*
> *and a healing remedy.*

The priest genuflects, takes the host and, holding it slightly raised above the paten or above the chalice, while facing the congregation, says aloud:

> *Behold the Lamb of God,*
> *behold Him who takes away the sins of the world.*
> *Blessed are those called to the supper of the Lamb.*

And together with the congregation says:

> *Lord, I am not worthy*
> *that You should enter under my roof,*
> *but only say the word*
> *and my soul shall be healed. (M)*

He turns towards the altar and says:

> *Body of Christ, preserve me for eternal life.*

He eats the Holy Communion and meanwhile the Communion hymn begins. He then takes the chalice and quietly says:

Blood of Christ, preserve me for eternal life.

And he drinks the Blood of Christ. After this, he takes the paten or ciborium and approaches the communicants. The priest raises a host slightly and shows it to each of the communicants, saying:

The Body of Christ.

The communicant replies:

Amen.

And receives Holy Communion.

(C) Communion is the peak of the Mass. We try to be one with the Father, and Son, and the Holy Spirit. God enters into us and expects of us that we enter into Him. We enter Him by concentrating all of our attention on Him. Mentally, we communicate to Him all that is in our hearts. Communion should be in total sincerity and openness of heart.

When the distribution of Communion is finished, the priest or the deacon cleans the paten over the chalice and cleans the chalice. He then returns to his seat. If possible, there should be a few moments of silence.

(C) Whether or not it is suitable is entirely up to the priest and usually depends on how he experienced this Communion.

POST COMMUNION PRAYER

Then, standing at the altar or at the chair and facing the people, with hands joined, the priest says:

Let us pray.

All pray in silence with the priest for a while, unless silence has just been observed. Then the priest, with extended hands, says the prayer after Communion,

God, to our weak nature, You are the only support.

Help our sick brothers and sisters,

that they may return healthy to Your church. (M)

Through Christ

(C) *Taken from the Mass for the Sick*

And the congregation says:

Amen.

THE CONCLUDING RITE

ANNOUNCEMENTS

If there is any information necessary for the congregation, it is read.

BLESSING

The priest himself, with hands joined and facing the congregation, says:

The Lord be with you

The congregation replies:

And with your spirit

The priest blesses the people with the words:

May Almighty God bless you, Father Son, and Holy Spirit.

The people reply:

Amen

DISMISSAL

Then, after this, the deacon or the priest himself, with joined hands, says to the congregation:

Go in peace.

The congregation replies:

Thanks be to God

Then the priest venerates the altar as usual with a kiss, as at the beginning. After making a profound bow with the ministers, he withdraws. If any liturgical action follows immediately, the rites of dismissal are omitted.

ABOUT THE AUTHOR

JOSIP LONČAR IS THE DIRECTOR of the foundation for the promotion of Christian values **Kristofori (in Croatia)** and the main editor of the monthly magazine **Book.** For many years now, he has been a member of Evangelization 2033 and attends regularly the Annual European Meetings of ACCSE - the Association of Coordinators of Catholic Schools of Evangelization. For many years, he was also the promotion officer of ICCRS (International Catholic Charismatic Renewal Services). For almost three decades he has held retreats in over 300 parishes in Croatia and abroad.

He is the author of the following titles:

The Charism of Faith; Grandmother's Rosary; Power from Above; How to Trust; School of Prayer (1, 2 and 3); I Want You to Live.

Lončar is the author of the film *Why Medjugorje?* which you can watch at: www.whymedugorje.org/index.html.

A WORD OF THANKS

I WOULD LIKE TO THANK Nikola, Erika, Mirjana, Ivan, Ksenija, Ivić and Krunoslav for the many hours we spent together reflecting on the Holy Mass.

I would like to thank Father Siniša, Father Remigije and Father Robert for their theological examination and suggestions which I readily accepted.

I would like to thank Mr. Albert Galea and his daughter Annabelle for their great help with English translation.

I would like to thank the late Bishop, Mons. Marko Culej, (died 19 August 2006), and my present Bishop, His Grace Rev. Fr. Marko Mrzljak, who has always encouraged me with his blessing and influenced me to continue growing in love towards God, the Church, and mankind.

I would also like to thank Cardinal Vinko Puljić for the Foreword that he wrote for the second edition of this book.

If there are fruits from this book, may the Lord recognise the merit that goes to these three Bishops.

My endless gratitude goes to our Lord, because from Him *"comes the will and to work for his good pleasure"* (Phil. 2:13).

Made in the USA
Middletown, DE
23 July 2023

35631357R00091